# Table of Contents

# INTRODUCTION

Are you tired of the same old boring meals day after day? Do you want to enjoy delicious food but struggle to find the time to cook? Well, say hello to your new best friend, the air fryer! This compact and powerful appliance is perfect for foodies on the go who want to enjoy their favorite meals without sacrificing precious time. With the air fryer, you can cook up a storm in minutes, and the best part? You don't even need to be a master chef to use it!

Take me myself as an example, I've always loved cooking, but sometimes the thought of preparing meals after a long day can be daunting. That's why I was so excited when I discovered the air fryer. It has completely revolutionized the way I cook and has become an essential tool in my kitchen.

When I first heard about the air fryer, I was skeptical. How could it possibly create crispy and flavorful food without the need for oil or frying? But once I tried it, I was hooked. I've been able to cook everything from chicken wings to vegetables to even desserts with ease and in a fraction of the time it would take using traditional cooking methods.

What's even better is that the air fryer allows you to enjoy your favorite foods in a healthier way. With little to no oil needed, you can indulge in crispy, flavorful dishes without the added calories and guilt that come with traditional frying methods.

That's why I decided to write this air frying cookbook - to share my favorite recipes and tips with others who are looking to make their cooking experience faster, easier, and more delicious. Whether you're a busy professional or a home cook looking for a new way to make your meals, the air fryer is the perfect tool to have in your kitchen.

In this cookbook, I will be sharing a variety of air fryer recipes, including classic comfort foods and healthier options. I want to show you just how versatile and convenient the air fryer can be. Even if you're not a cooking expert, you'll be able to follow along with the simple instructions and create delicious meals in no time.

I'm confident that you'll love the convenience and versatility of the air fryer as much as I do. It has completely changed the way I approach cooking and has allowed me to enjoy delicious meals without the added stress and time commitment. So, get ready to upgrade your cooking game and say hello to your new kitchen bestie - the air fryer!

# The Air Fryer - Your New Best Friend in the Kitchen

## What is Air Fryer

Air fryers have taken the cooking world by storm in recent years, but what exactly is an air fryer? Essentially, an air fryer is a small convection oven that sits on your countertop. Instead of cooking your food in hot oil like a deep fryer, an air fryer circulates hot air around the food, cooking it to crispy perfection. By doing so, it eliminates the need for excessive oil, reducing the overall fat content of your food. In fact, using an air fryer can reduce the amount of fat in your food by up to 75 percent compared to traditional frying methods.

But air fryers are not just for frying. They can also be used to grill, roast, and bake a variety of foods. You can use them to cook everything from chicken wings to vegetables, and even desserts like donuts and brownies. Plus, because they use hot air rather than oil, they produce less smoke and odor than traditional frying methods, making them a great option for indoor cooking.

## The History of Air Fryer

While air fryers may seem like a recent invention, the truth is that they have been around for quite some time. In fact, the idea of cooking with hot air has been around since the 1940s. French engineers developed a technique for cooking food using hot air, and this idea was further developed over the years.

However, it wasn't until 2010 that the first air fryer was introduced to the market. This initial model was quite basic, with limited functionality and a small cooking capacity. But over time, air fryers have become increasingly advanced, with new features and technology that make them even more versatile and convenient.

Today, air fryers come in a variety of shapes and sizes, with different features and cooking capacities to suit different needs. Some models even come with accessories like grill pans and baking trays, allowing you to use your air fryer for even more cooking tasks.

## Why Air Fryer Became So Popular Today

Air fryers have become a staple in many kitchens around the world, and it's easy to see why. In this section, we'll explore the benefits that have made them so popular, from their health benefits to their versatility and convenience.

1.Healthier Cooking: One of the biggest benefits of using an air fryer is that it allows you to cook food with little to no oil. This makes it a great option for those who are looking to cut back on calories or follow a healthier diet.

2.Versatility: Air fryers can be used to cook a wide variety of foods, from chicken wings and french fries to vegetables and even desserts. Some models even come with accessories like grill pans and baking trays, making them even more versatile.

3.Convenience: Air fryers are incredibly easy to use, with simple controls that allow you to adjust the temperature and cooking time with ease. Plus, they cook food quickly, which means you can have a healthy and delicious meal on the table in no time.

4.Crispy Texture: Air fryers use hot air to cook food, which results in a crispy texture that is similar to fried food. This means you can enjoy the taste and texture of fried food without the added oil and fat.

5.Easy to Clean: Most air fryers come with removable baskets and non-stick surfaces, making them incredibly easy to clean. Simply remove the basket, wash it with soap and water, and you're done.

6.Reduced Odor: Because air fryers use hot air rather than oil, they produce less smoke and odor than traditional frying methods. This makes them a great option for indoor cooking.

7.Saves Space: Air fryers are typically small and compact, which means they take up less space in your kitchen than traditional cooking appliances like ovens and deep fryers. This makes them a great option for those who have limited counter space or live in small apartments.

## Maximizing Your Air Fryer's Potential

Now that you know the basics of air fryers and why they're so great, it's time to start cooking! In this section, I'll provide some practical tips and tricks for using your air fryer to its full potential.

1.Use Baking Powder to Get a Crispy Coating: For an extra crispy coating on foods like chicken wings or fish, try adding a pinch of baking powder to your breading mixture. The baking powder helps to create a light, crispy texture when combined with the heat of the air fryer.

2.Try Grilling in Your Air Fryer: Some air fryer models come with a grilling feature, allowing you to grill foods like burgers, hot dogs, or vegetables. This feature can be a great way to get that grilled flavor without having to leave your kitchen.

3.Use Skewers for Kebabs and More: If you're looking to cook foods like kebabs or small vegetables in your air fryer, try using skewers to keep everything in place. Skewers can help ensure that your food cooks evenly and stays in place while inside the air fryer basket.

4.Use Foil to Make Packets: For foods like fish or vegetables that can benefit from steaming, try making foil packets, Place your food and any seasonings or sauces into a foil packet, and then place the packet into the air fryer basket. The steam created inside the packet helps to keep your food moist and flavorful.

5.Make Your Own Marinades: To add flavor to your air fryer meals, consider making your own marinades using ingredients like garlic, lemon, herbs, and spices. Simply marinate your protein for a few hours or overnight before cooking in the air fryer for a delicious and flavorful result.

## Start Air Frying Today!

The air fryer revolution has arrived, and there's no better time to jump on board. By using an air fryer, you can enjoy the delicious taste and texture of fried foods without the added fat and calories. With a few simple tips and tricks, you can maximize your air fryer's potential and create healthy and tasty meals for you and your family. So what are you waiting for? Start air frying today!

# Chapter 1 Breakfasts

# Chapter 1 Breakfasts

## Sirloin Steaks with Eggs

**Prep time: 8 minutes | Cook time: 14 minutes per batch | Serves 4**

Cooking oil spray

4 (110 g) sirloin steaks

1 teaspoon granulated garlic, divided

1 teaspoon salt, divided

1 teaspoon freshly ground black pepper, divided

4 eggs

½ teaspoon paprika

1. Insert the crisper plate into the basket and the basket into the unit. Preheat the unit by selecting AIR FRY, setting the temperature to 180ºC, and setting the time to 3 minutes. Select START/STOP to begin. 2. Once the unit is preheated, spray the crisper plate with cooking oil. Place 2 steaks into the basket; do not oil or season them at this time. 3. Select AIR FRY, set the temperature to 180ºC, and set the time to 9 minutes. Select START/STOP to begin. 4. After 5 minutes, open the unit and flip the steaks. Sprinkle each with ¼ teaspoon of granulated garlic, ¼ teaspoon of salt, and ¼ teaspoon of pepper. Resume cooking until the steaks register at least 64ºC on a food thermometer. 5. When the cooking is complete, transfer the steaks to a plate and tent with aluminum foil to keep warm. Repeat steps 2, 3, and 4 with the remaining steaks. 6. Spray 4 ramekins with rapeseed oil. Crack 1 egg into each ramekin. Sprinkle the eggs with the paprika and remaining ½ teaspoon each of salt and pepper. Working in batches, place 2 ramekins into the basket. 7. Select BAKE, set the temperature to 170ºC, and set the time to 5 minutes. Select START/STOP to begin. 8. When the cooking is complete and the eggs are cooked to 72ºC, remove the ramekins and repeat step 7 with the remaining 2 ramekins. 9. Serve the eggs with the steaks.

## Tomato and Mozzarella Bruschetta

**Prep time: 5 minutes | Cook time: 4 minutes | Serves 1**

6 small loaf slices

120 g tomatoes, finely chopped

85 g Cheddar cheese, grated

1 tablespoon fresh basil, chopped

1 tablespoon rapeseed oil

1. Preheat the air fryer to 180ºC. 2. Put the loaf slices inside the air fryer and air fry for about 3 minutes. 3. Add the tomato, Mozzarella, basil, and rapeseed oil on top. 4. Air fry for an additional minute before serving.

## Bacon Cheese Egg with Avocado

**Prep time: 15 minutes | Cook time: 20 minutes | Serves 4**

6 large eggs

60 ml double cream

350 g chopped cauliflower

235 g grated medium Cheddar cheese

1 medium avocado, peeled and pitted

8 tablespoons full-fat sour cream

2 spring onions, sliced on the bias

12 slices bacon, cooked and crumbled

1. In a medium bowl, whisk eggs and cream together. Pour into a round baking dish. 2. Add cauliflower and mix, then top with Cheddar. Place dish into the air fryer basket. 3. Adjust the temperature to 160ºC and set the timer for 20 minutes. 4. When completely cooked, eggs will be firm and cheese will be browned. Slice into four pieces. 5. Slice avocado and divide evenly among pieces. Top each piece with 2 tablespoons sour cream, sliced spring onions, and crumbled bacon.

## Buffalo Egg Cups

**Prep time: 10 minutes | Cook time: 15 minutes | Serves 2**

4 large eggs

60 g full-fat soft cheese

2 tablespoons buffalo sauce

120 g grated mature Cheddar cheese

1. Crack eggs into two ramekins. 2. In a small microwave-safe bowl, mix soft cheese, buffalo sauce, and Cheddar. Microwave for 20 seconds and then stir. Place a spoonful into each ramekin on top of the eggs. 3. Place ramekins into the air fryer basket. 4. Adjust the temperature to 160ºC and bake for 15 minutes. 5. Serve warm.

# Breakfast Sausage and Cauliflower

**Prep time: 5 minutes | Cook time: 45 minutes | Serves 4**

450 g sausage meat, cooked and crumbled

475 ml double/whipping cream

1 head cauliflower, chopped

235 g grated Cheddar cheese,

plus more for topping

8 eggs, beaten

Salt and ground black pepper, to taste

1. Preheat the air fryer to 180°C. 2. In a large bowl, mix the sausage, cream, chopped cauliflower, cheese and eggs. Sprinkle with salt and ground black pepper. 3. Pour the mixture into a greased casserole dish. Bake in the preheated air fryer for 45 minutes or until firm. 4. Top with more Cheddar cheese and serve.

# Apple Rolls

**Prep time: 20 minutes | Cook time: 20 to 24 minutes | Makes 12 rolls**

Apple Rolls:

235 g plain flour, plus more for dusting

2 tablespoons granulated sugar

1 teaspoon salt

3 tablespoons butter, at room temperature

180 ml milk, whole or semi-skimmed

95 g packed light soft brown

sugar

1 teaspoon ground cinnamon

1 large Granny Smith apple, peeled and diced

1 to 2 tablespoons oil

Icing:

75 g icing sugar

½ teaspoon vanilla extract

2 to 3 tablespoons milk, whole or semi-skimmed

Make the Apple Rolls 1. In a large bowl, whisk the flour, granulated sugar, and salt until blended. Stir in the butter and milk briefly until a sticky dough forms. 2. In a small bowl, stir together the soft brown sugar, cinnamon, and apple. 3. Place a piece of parchment paper on a work surface and dust it with flour. Roll the dough on the prepared surface to ¼ inch thickness. 4. Spread the apple mixture over the dough. Roll up the dough jelly roll-style, pinching the ends to seal. Cut the dough into 12 rolls. 5. Preheat the air fryer to 160°C. 6. Line the air fryer basket with parchment paper and spritz it with oil. Place 6 rolls on the prepared parchment 7. Bake for 5 minutes. Flip the rolls and bake for 5 to 7 minutes more until lightly browned. Repeat with the remaining rolls. Make the Icing 8. In a medium bowl, whisk the icing sugar, vanilla, and milk until blended. 9. Drizzle over the warm rolls.

# Green Eggs and Ham

**Prep time: 5 minutes | Cook time: 10 minutes | Serves 2**

1 large Hass avocado, halved and pitted

2 thin slices ham

2 large eggs

2 tablespoons chopped spring onions, plus more for garnish

½ teaspoon fine sea salt

¼ teaspoon ground black pepper

60 g grated Cheddar cheese (omit for dairy-free)

1. Preheat the air fryer to 200°C. 2. Place a slice of ham into the cavity of each avocado half. Crack an egg on top of the ham, then sprinkle on the green onions, salt, and pepper. 3. Place the avocado halves in the air fryer cut side up and air fry for 10 minutes, or until the egg is cooked to your desired doneness. Top with the cheese (if using) and air fry for 30 seconds more, or until the cheese is melted. Garnish with chopped green onions. 4. Best served fresh. Store extras in an airtight container in the fridge for up to 4 days. Reheat in a preheated 180°C air fryer for a few minutes, until warmed through.

# Mozzarella Bacon Calzones

**Prep time: 15 minutes | Cook time: 12 minutes | Serves 4**

2 large eggs

120 g blanched finely ground almond flour

475 g grated Cheddar cheese

60 g soft cheese, softened and broken into small pieces

4 slices cooked bacon, crumbled

1. Beat eggs in a small bowl. Pour into a medium nonstick skillet over medium heat and scramble. Set aside. 2. In a large microwave-safe bowl, mix flour and Mozzarella. Add soft cheese to the bowl. 3. Place bowl in microwave and cook 45 seconds on high to melt cheese, then stir with a fork until a soft dough ball forms. 4. Cut a piece of parchment to fit air fryer basket. Separate dough into two sections and press each out into an 8-inch round. 5. On half of each dough round, place half of the scrambled eggs and crumbled bacon. Fold the other side of the dough over and press to seal the edges. 6. Place calzones on ungreased parchment and into air fryer basket. Adjust the temperature to 180°C and set the timer for 12 minutes, turning calzones halfway through cooking. Crust will be golden and firm when done. 7. Let calzones cool on a cooking rack 5 minutes before serving.

## Breakfast Pitta

**Prep time: 5 minutes | Cook time: 6 minutes | Serves 2**

| | |
|---|---|
| 1 wholemeal pitta | ¼ teaspoon dried oregano |
| 2 teaspoons rapeseed oil | ¼ teaspoon dried thyme |
| ½ shallot, diced | ⅛ teaspoon salt |
| ¼ teaspoon garlic, minced | 2 tablespoons grated Parmesan |
| 1 large egg | cheese |

1. Preheat the air fryer to 190ºC. 2. Brush the top of the pitta with rapeseed oil, then spread the diced shallot and minced garlic over the pitta. 3. Crack the egg into a small bowl or ramekin, and season it with oregano, thyme, and salt. 4. Place the pitta into the air fryer basket, and gently pour the egg onto the top of the pitta. Sprinkle with cheese over the top. 5. Bake for 6 minutes. 6. Allow to cool for 5 minutes before cutting into pieces for serving.

## Turkey Sausage Breakfast Pizza

**Prep time: 15 minutes | Cook time: 24 minutes | Serves 2**

| | |
|---|---|
| 4 large eggs, divided | 120 g grated low-moisture |
| 1 tablespoon water | Mozzarella or other melting |
| ½ teaspoon garlic powder | cheese |
| ½ teaspoon onion granules | 1 link cooked turkey sausage, |
| ½ teaspoon dried oregano | chopped (about 60 g) |
| 2 tablespoons coconut flour | 2 sun-dried tomatoes, finely |
| 3 tablespoons grated Parmesan | chopped |
| cheese | 2 spring onions, thinly sliced |

1. Preheat the air fryer to 200ºC. Line a cake pan with parchment paper and lightly coat the paper with rapeseed oil. 2. In a large bowl, whisk 2 of the eggs with the water, garlic powder, onion granules, and dried oregano. Add the coconut flour, breaking up any lumps with your hands as you add it to the bowl. Stir the coconut flour into the egg mixture, mixing until smooth. Stir in the Parmesan cheese. Allow the mixture to rest for a few minutes until thick and dough-like. 3. Transfer the mixture to the prepared pan. Use a spatula to spread it evenly and slightly up the sides of the pan. Air fry until the crust is set but still light in color, about 10 minutes. Top with the cheeses, sausage, and sun-dried tomatoes. 4. Break the remaining 2 eggs into a small bowl, then slide them onto the pizza. Return the pizza to the air fryer. Air fry 10 to 14 minutes until the egg whites are set and the yolks are the desired doneness. Top with the scallions and allow to rest for 5 minutes before serving.

## Broccoli-Mushroom Frittata

**Prep time: 10 minutes | Cook time: 20 minutes | Serves 2**

| | |
|---|---|
| 1 tablespoon rapeseed oil | ½ teaspoon salt |
| 350 g broccoli florets, finely | ¼ teaspoon freshly ground |
| chopped | black pepper |
| 120 g sliced brown mushrooms | 6 eggs |
| 60 g finely chopped onion | 60 g Parmesan cheese |

1. In a nonstick cake pan, combine the rapeseed oil, broccoli, mushrooms, onion, salt, and pepper. Stir until the vegetables are thoroughly coated with oil. Place the cake pan in the air fryer basket and set the air fryer to 200ºC. Air fry for 5 minutes until the vegetables soften. 2. Meanwhile, in a medium bowl, whisk the eggs and Parmesan until thoroughly combined. Pour the egg mixture into the pan and shake gently to distribute the vegetables. Air fry for another 15 minutes until the eggs are set. 3. Remove from the air fryer and let sit for 5 minutes to cool slightly. Use a silicone spatula to gently lift the frittata onto a plate before serving.

## Banana-Nut Muffins

**Prep time: 5 minutes | Cook time: 15 minutes | Makes 10 muffins**

| | |
|---|---|
| Oil, for spraying | 1 large egg |
| 2 very ripe bananas | 1 teaspoon vanilla extract |
| 95 g packed light soft brown | 90 g plain flour |
| sugar | 1 teaspoon baking powder |
| 80 ml rapeseed oil or vegetable | 1 teaspoon ground cinnamon |
| oil | 120 g chopped walnuts |

1. Preheat the air fryer to 160ºC. Spray 10 silicone muffin cups lightly with oil. 2. In a medium bowl, mash the bananas. Add the soft brown sugar, rapeseed oil, egg, and vanilla and stir to combine. 3. Fold in the flour, baking powder, and cinnamon until just combined. 4. Add the walnuts and fold a few times to distribute throughout the batter. 5. Divide the batter equally among the prepared muffin cups and place them in the basket. You may need to work in batches, depending on the size of your air fryer. 6. Cook for 15 minutes, or until golden brown and a toothpick inserted into the center of a muffin comes out clean. The air fryer tends to brown muffins more than the oven, so don't be alarmed if they are darker than you're used to. They will still taste great. 7. Let cool on a wire rack before serving.

## Sausage and Cheese Balls

Prep time: 10 minutes | Cook time: 12 minutes |
Makes 16 balls

| | |
|---|---|
| 450 g pork sausage meat, removed from casings | 30 g full-fat soft cheese, softened |
| 120 g grated Cheddar cheese | 1 large egg |

1. Mix all ingredients in a large bowl. Form into sixteen (1-inch) balls. Place the balls into the air fryer basket. 2. Adjust the temperature to 200°C and air fry for 12 minutes. 3. Shake the basket two or three times during cooking. Sausage balls will be browned on the outside and have an internal temperature of at least 64°C when completely cooked. 4. Serve warm.

## Peppered Maple Bacon Knots

Prep time: 5 minutes | Cook time: 7 to 8 minutes |
Serves 6

| | |
|---|---|
| 450 g maple smoked/cured bacon rashers | 48 g soft brown sugar |
| 60 ml maple syrup | Coarsely cracked black peppercorns, to taste |

1. Preheat the air fryer to 200°C. 2. On a clean work surface, tie each bacon strip in a loose knot. 3. Stir together the maple syrup and soft brown sugar in a bowl. Generously brush this mixture over the bacon knots. 4. Working in batches, arrange the bacon knots in the air fryer basket. Sprinkle with the coarsely cracked black peppercorns. 5. Air fry for 5 minutes. Flip the bacon knots and continue cooking for 2 to 3 minutes more, or until the bacon is crisp. 6. Remove from the basket to a paper towel-lined plate. Repeat with the remaining bacon knots. 7. Let the bacon knots cool for a few minutes and serve warm.

## Simple Cinnamon Toasts

Prep time: 5 minutes | Cook time: 4 minutes | Serves 4

| | |
|---|---|
| 1 tablespoon salted butter | ½ teaspoon vanilla extract |
| 2 teaspoons ground cinnamon | 10 bread slices |
| 4 tablespoons sugar | |

1. Preheat the air fryer to 190°C. 2. In a bowl, combine the butter, cinnamon, sugar, and vanilla extract. Spread onto the slices of bread. 3. Put the bread inside the air fryer and bake for 4 minutes or until golden brown. 4. Serve warm.

## Baked Potato Breakfast Boats

Prep time: 10 minutes | Cook time: 20 minutes |
Serves 4

| | |
|---|---|
| 2 large white potatoes, scrubbed | 4 eggs |
| rapeseed oil | 2 tablespoons chopped, cooked |
| Salt and freshly ground black pepper, to taste | bacon |
| | 235 g grated Cheddar cheese |

1. Poke holes in the potatoes with a fork and microwave on full power for 5 minutes. 2. Turn potatoes over and cook an additional 3 to 5 minutes, or until the potatoes are fork-tender. 3. Cut the potatoes in half lengthwise and use a spoon to scoop out the inside of the potato. Be careful to leave a layer of potato so that it makes a sturdy "boat." 4. Preheat the air fryer to 180°C. 5. Lightly spray the air fryer basket with rapeseed oil. Spray the skin side of the potatoes with oil and sprinkle with salt and pepper to taste. 6. Place the potato skins in the air fryer basket, skin-side down. Crack one egg into each potato skin. 7. Sprinkle ½ tablespoon of bacon pieces and 60 ml grated cheese on top of each egg. Sprinkle with salt and pepper to taste. 8. Air fry until the yolk is slightly runny, 5 to 6 minutes, or until the yolk is fully cooked, 7 to 10 minutes.

## Homemade Toaster Pastries

Prep time: 10 minutes | Cook time: 11 minutes |
Makes 6 pastries

| | |
|---|---|
| Oil, for spraying | 340 g icing sugar |
| 1 (425 g) package ready-to-roll pie crust | 3 tablespoons milk |
| | 1 to 2 tablespoons sprinkles of choice |
| 6 tablespoons jam or preserves of choice | |

1. Preheat the air fryer to 180°C. Line the air fryer basket with parchment and lightly spray with oil. 2. Cut the pie crust into 12 rectangles, about 3 by 4 inches each. You will need to reroll the dough scraps to get 12 rectangles. 3. Spread 1 tablespoon of jam in the centre of 6 rectangles, leaving ¼ inch around the edges. 4. Pour some water into a small bowl. Use your finger to moisten the edge of each rectangle. 5. Top each rectangle with another and use your fingers to press around the edges. Using the prongs of a fork, seal the edges of the dough and poke a few holes in the top of each one. Place the pastries in the prepared basket. 6. Air fry for 11 minutes. Let cool completely. 7. In a medium bowl, whisk together the icing sugar and milk. Spread the icing over the tops of the pastries and add sprinkles. Serve immediately.

## Turkey Breakfast Sausage Patties

**Prep time: 5 minutes | Cook time: 10 minutes |**
**Serves 4**

| | |
|---|---|
| 1 tablespoon chopped fresh thyme | ½ teaspoon onion granules |
| 1 tablespoon chopped fresh sage | ½ teaspoon garlic powder |
| 1¼ teaspoons coarse or flaky salt | ⅛ teaspoon crushed red pepper flakes |
| 1 teaspoon chopped fennel seeds | ⅛ teaspoon freshly ground black pepper |
| ¾ teaspoon smoked paprika | 450 g lean turkey mince |
| | 120 g finely minced sweet apple (peeled) |

1. Thoroughly combine the thyme, sage, salt, fennel seeds, paprika, onion granules, garlic powder, red pepper flakes, and black pepper in a medium bowl. 2. Add the turkey mince and apple and stir until well incorporated. Divide the mixture into 8 equal portions and shape into patties with your hands, each about ¼ inch thick and 3 inches in diameter. 3. Preheat the air fryer to 200ºC. 4. Place the patties in the air fryer basket in a single layer. You may need to work in batches to avoid overcrowding. 5. Air fry for 5 minutes. Flip the patties and air fry for 5 minutes, or until the patties are nicely browned and cooked through. 6. Remove from the basket to a plate and repeat with the remaining patties. 7. Serve warm.

## Greek Bagels

**Prep time: 10 minutes | Cook time: 10 minutes |**
**Makes 2 bagels**

| | |
|---|---|
| 60 g self-raising flour, plus more for dusting | 4 teaspoons sesame seeds or za'atar |
| 120 ml natural yoghurt | Cooking oil spray |
| 1 egg | 1 tablespoon butter, melted |
| 1 tablespoon water | |

1. In a large bowl, using a wooden spoon, stir together the flour and yoghurt until a tacky dough forms. Transfer the dough to a lightly floured work surface and roll the dough into a ball. 2. Cut the dough into 2 pieces and roll each piece into a log. Form each log into a bagel shape, pinching the ends together. 3. In a small bowl, whisk the egg and water. Brush the egg wash on the bagels. 4. Sprinkle 2 teaspoons of the toppings on each bagel and gently press it into the dough. 5. Insert the crisper plate into the basket and the basket into the unit. Preheat the unit by selecting BAKE, setting the temperature to 170ºC, and setting the time to 3 minutes. Select START/STOP to begin. 6. Once the unit is preheated, spray the crisper plate with cooking spray. Drizzle the bagels with the butter and place them into the basket. 7. Select BAKE, set the temperature to 170ºC, and set the time to 10 minutes. Select START/STOP to begin. 8. When the cooking is complete, the bagels should be lightly golden on the outside. Serve warm.

## Sausage Egg Cup

**Prep time: 10 minutes | Cook time: 15 minutes |**
**Serves 6**

| | |
|---|---|
| 340 g pork sausage, removed from casings | ¼ teaspoon ground black pepper |
| 6 large eggs | ½ teaspoon crushed red pepper flakes |
| ½ teaspoon salt | |

1. Place sausage in six 4-inch ramekins (about 60 g per ramekin) greased with cooking oil. Press sausage down to cover bottom and about ½-inch up the sides of ramekins. Crack one egg into each ramekin and sprinkle evenly with salt, black pepper, and red pepper flakes. 2. Place ramekins into air fryer basket. Adjust the temperature to 180ºC and set the timer for 15 minutes. Egg cups will be done when sausage is fully cooked to at least 64ºC and the egg is firm. Serve warm.

## Wholemeal Banana-Walnut Bread

**Prep time: 10 minutes | Cook time: 23 minutes |**
**Serves 6**

| | |
|---|---|
| rapeseed oil cooking spray | 2 tablespoons honey |
| 2 ripe medium bananas | 120 g wholemeal flour |
| 1 large egg | ¼ teaspoon salt |
| 60 ml non-fat natural yoghurt | ¼ teaspoon baking soda |
| 60 ml rapeseed oil | ½ teaspoon ground cinnamon |
| ½ teaspoon vanilla extract | 60 g chopped walnuts |

1. Preheat the air fryer to 180ºC. Lightly coat the inside of a 8-by-4-inch loaf pan with rapeseed oil cooking spray. (Or use two 5 ½-by-3-inch loaf pans.) 2. In a large bowl, mash the bananas with a fork. Add the egg, yoghurt, rapeseed oil, vanilla, and honey. Mix until well combined and mostly smooth. 3. Sift the wholemeal flour, salt, baking soda, and cinnamon into the wet mixture, then stir until just combined. Do not overmix. 4. Gently fold in the walnuts. 5. Pour into the prepared loaf pan and spread to distribute evenly. 6. Place the loaf pan in the air fryer basket and bake for 20 to 23 minutes, or until golden brown on top and a toothpick inserted into the center comes out clean. 7. Allow to cool for 5 minutes before serving.

## Bacon Eggs on the Go

### Prep time: 5 minutes | Cook time: 15 minutes | Serves 1

2 eggs

110 g bacon, cooked

Salt and ground black pepper, to taste

1. Preheat the air fryer to 200ºC. Put liners in a regular cupcake tin. 2. Crack an egg into each of the cups and add the bacon. Season with some pepper and salt. 3. Bake in the preheated air fryer for 15 minutes, or until the eggs are set. Serve warm.

## Keto Quiche

### Prep time: 10 minutes | Cook time: 1 hour | Makes 1 (6-inch) quiche

Crust:

150 g blanched almond flour

300 g grated Parmesan or Gouda cheese

¼ teaspoon fine sea salt

1 large egg, beaten

Filling:

120 g chicken or beef stock (or vegetable stock for vegetarian)

235 g grated Swiss cheese (about 110 g)

110 g soft cheese (120 ml)

1 tablespoon unsalted butter, melted

4 large eggs, beaten

80 g minced leeks or sliced spring onions

¾ teaspoon fine sea salt

⅛ teaspoon cayenne pepper

Chopped spring onions, for garnish

1. Preheat the air fryer to 160ºC. Grease a pie pan. Spray two large pieces of parchment paper with avocado oil and set them on the countertop. 2. Make the crust: In a medium-sized bowl, combine the flour, cheese, and salt and mix well. Add the egg and mix until the dough is well combined and stiff. 3. Place the dough in the center of one of the greased pieces of parchment. Top with the other piece of parchment. Using a rolling pin, roll out the dough into a circle about 1/16 inch thick. 4. Press the pie crust into the prepared pie pan. Place it in the air fryer and bake for 12 minutes, or until it starts to lightly brown. 5. While the crust bakes, make the filling: In a large bowl, combine the stock, Swiss cheese, soft cheese, and butter. Stir in the eggs, leeks, salt, and cayenne pepper. When the crust is ready, pour the mixture into the crust, 6. Place the quiche in the air fryer and bake for 15 minutes. Turn the heat down to 150ºC and bake for an additional 30 minutes, or until a knife inserted 1 inch from the edge comes out clean. You may have to cover the edges of the crust with foil to prevent burning. 7. Allow the quiche to cool for 10 minutes before garnishing it with chopped spring onions and cutting it into wedges. 8. Store leftovers in an airtight container in the refrigerator for up to 4 days or in the freezer for up to a month. Reheat in a preheated 180ºC air fryer for a few minutes, until warmed through.

## Red Pepper and Feta Frittata

### Prep time: 10 minutes | Cook time: 20 minutes | Serves 4

rapeseed oil cooking spray

8 large eggs

1 medium red pepper, diced

½ teaspoon salt

½ teaspoon black pepper

1 garlic clove, minced

120 g feta, divided

1. Preheat the air fryer to 180ºC. Lightly coat the inside of a 6-inch round cake pan with rapeseed oil cooking spray. 2. In a large bowl, beat the eggs for 1 to 2 minutes, or until well combined. 3. Add the red pepper, salt, black pepper, and garlic to the eggs, and mix together until the red pepper is distributed throughout. 4. Fold in 60 ml the feta cheese. 5. Pour the egg mixture into the prepared cake pan, and sprinkle the remaining 60 ml feta over the top. 6. Place into the air fryer and bake for 18 to 20 minutes, or until the eggs are set in the center. 7. Remove from the air fryer and allow to cool for 5 minutes before serving.

## Jalapeño and Bacon Breakfast Pizza

### Prep time: 5 minutes | Cook time: 10 minutes | Serves 2

235 ml grated Cheddar cheese

30 g soft cheese, broken into small pieces

4 slices cooked bacon, chopped

60 g chopped pickled jalapeños

1 large egg, whisked

¼ teaspoon salt

1. Place Mozzarella in a single layer on the bottom of an ungreased round nonstick baking dish. Scatter soft cheese pieces, bacon, and jalapeños over Mozzarella, then pour egg evenly around baking dish. 2. Sprinkle with salt and place into air fryer basket. Adjust the temperature to 170ºC and bake for 10 minutes. When cheese is brown and egg is set, pizza will be done. 3. Let cool on a large plate 5 minutes before serving.

## Chapter 2 Family Favorites

# Chapter 2 Family Favorites

## Cajun Shrimp

**Prep time: 15 minutes | Cook time: 9 minutes | Serves 4**

Oil, for spraying
450 g king prawns, peeled and deveined
1 tablespoon Cajun seasoning
170 g Polish sausage, cut into thick slices
½ medium courgette, cut into ¼-inch-thick slices

½ medium yellow squash or butternut squash, cut into ¼-inch-thick slices
1 green pepper, seeded and cut into 1-inch pieces
2 tablespoons olive oil
½ teaspoon salt

1. Preheat the air fryer to 200ºC.2.Line the air fryer basket with parchment and spray lightly with oil. In a large bowl, toss together the shrimp and Cajun seasoning.3.Add the kielbasa, courgette, squash, pepper, olive oil, and salt and mix well.4.Transfer the mixture to the prepared basket, taking care not to overcrowd.5.You may need to work in batches, depending on the size of your air fryer.6.Cook for 9 minutes, shaking and stirring every 3 minutes.7.Serve immediately.

## Chinese-Inspired Spareribs

**Prep time: 30 minutes | Cook time: 8 minutes | Serves 4**

Oil, for spraying
340 g pork ribs, cut into 3-inch-long pieces
235 ml soy sauce
140 g sugar

120 g beef broth
60 ml honey
2 tablespoons minced garlic
1 teaspoon ground ginger
2 drops red food dye (optional)

1. Line the air fryer basket with parchment and spray lightly with oil. 2.Combine the ribs, soy sauce, sugar, beef broth, honey, garlic, ginger, and food colouring (if using) in a large zip-top plastic bag, seal, and shake well until completely coated. 3.Refrigerate for at least 30 minutes. 4.Place the ribs in the prepared basket. 5.Air fry at 190ºC for 8 minutes, or until the internal temperature reaches 74ºC.

## Steak Tips and Potatoes

**Prep time: 10 minutes | Cook time: 20 minutes | Serves 4**

Oil, for spraying
227 g baby potatoes, cut in half
½ teaspoon salt
450 g steak, cut into ½-inch pieces

1 teaspoon Worcester sauce
1 teaspoon garlic powder
½ teaspoon salt
½ teaspoon ground black pepper

1. Line the air fryer basket with parchment and spray lightly with oil. 2.In a microwave-safe bowl, combine the potatoes and salt, then pour in about ½ inch of water. 3.Microwave for 7 minutes, or until the potatoes are nearly tender. Drain. 4.In a large bowl, gently mix together the steak, potatoes, Worcester sauce, garlic, salt, and black pepper. 5.Spread the mixture in an even layer in the prepared basket. Air fry at 200ºC for 12 to 17 minutes, stirring after 5 to 6 minutes. 6.The cooking time will depend on the thickness of the meat and preferred doneness.

## Fish and Vegetable Tacos

**Prep time: 15 minutes | Cook time: 9 to 12 minutes | Serves 4**

450 g white fish fillets, such as sole or cod
2 teaspoons olive oil
3 tablespoons freshly squeezed lemon juice, divided
350 g chopped red cabbage

1 large carrot, grated
120 ml low-salt salsa
80 ml low-fat Greek yoghurt
4 soft low-salt wholemeal tortillas

1. Brush the fish with the olive oil and sprinkle with 1 tablespoon of lemon juice. 2.Air fry in the air fryer basket at 200ºC for 9 to 12 minutes, or until the fish just flakes when tested with a fork. 3.Meanwhile, in a medium bowl, stir together the remaining 2 tablespoons of lemon juice, the red cabbage, carrot, salsa, and yoghurt. 4.When the fish is cooked, remove it from the air fryer basket and break it up into large pieces. 5.Offer the fish, tortillas, and the cabbage mixture, and let each person assemble a taco.

## Meringue Cookies

**Prep time: 15 minutes | Cook time: 1 hour 30 minutes | Makes 20 cookies**

Oil, for spraying

4 large egg whites

185 g sugar

Pinch cream of tartar

1. Preheat the air fryer to 60ºC. 2.Line the air fryer basket with parchment and spray lightly with oil. 3.In a small heatproof bowl, whisk together the egg whites and sugar. 4.Fill a small saucepan halfway with water, place it over medium heat, and bring to a light simmer. 5.Place the bowl with the egg whites on the saucepan, making sure the bottom of the bowl does not touch the water. 6.Whisk the mixture until the sugar is dissolved. Transfer the mixture to a large bowl and add the cream of tartar. 7.Using an electric mixer, beat the mixture on high until it is glossy and stiff peaks form. 8.Transfer the mixture to a piping bag or a zip-top plastic bag with a corner cut off. Pipe rounds into the prepared basket. 9.You may need to work in batches, depending on the size of your air fryer. Cook for 1 hour 30 minutes. 10.Turn off the air fryer and let the meringues cool completely inside. 11.The residual heat will continue to dry them out.

## Puffed Egg Tarts

**Prep time: 10 minutes | Cook time: 42 minutes | Makes 4 tarts**

Oil, for spraying

Plain flour, for dusting

1 (340 g) sheet frozen puff pastry, thawed

180 g shredded Cheddar cheese, divided

4 large eggs

2 teaspoons chopped fresh parsley

Salt and ground black pepper, to taste

1. Preheat the air fryer to 200ºC. 2.Line the air fryer basket with parchment and spray lightly with oil. Lightly dust your work surface with flour. 3.Unfold the puff pastry and cut it into 4 equal squares. 4.Place 2 squares in the prepared basket. Cook for 10 minutes. 5.Remove the basket. Press the centre of each tart shell with a spoon to make an indentation. 6.Sprinkle 3 tablespoons of cheese into each indentation and crack 1 egg into the centre of each tart shell. 7.Cook for another 7 to 11 minutes, or until the eggs are cooked to your desired doneness. 8.Repeat with the remaining puff pastry squares, cheese, and eggs. 9.Sprinkle evenly with the parsley, and season with salt and black pepper. 10.Serve immediately.

## Fried Green Tomatoes

**Prep time: 15 minutes | Cook time: 6 to 8 minutes | Serves 4**

4 medium green tomatoes

50 g plain flour

2 egg whites

60 ml almond milk

235 g ground almonds

120 g Japanese breadcrumbs

2 teaspoons olive oil

1 teaspoon paprika

1 clove garlic, minced

1. Rinse the tomatoes and pat dry. 2.Cut the tomatoes into ½-inch slices, discarding the thinner ends. Put the flour on a plate. 3.In a shallow bowl, beat the egg whites with the almond milk until frothy. 4.And on another plate, combine the almonds, breadcrumbs, olive oil, paprika, and garlic and mix well. 5.Dip the tomato slices into the flour, then into the egg white mixture, then into the almond mixture to coat. 6.Place four of the coated tomato slices in the air fryer basket. 7.Air fry at 200ºC for 6 to 8 minutes or until the tomato coating is crisp and golden brown. 8.Repeat with remaining tomato slices and serve immediately.

## Filo Vegetable Triangles

**Prep time: 15 minutes | Cook time: 6 to 11 minutes | Serves 6**

3 tablespoons finely chopped onion

2 garlic cloves, minced

2 tablespoons grated carrot

1 teaspoon olive oil

3 tablespoons frozen baby peas, thawed

2 tablespoons fat-free soft white cheese, at room temperature

6 sheets frozen filo pastry, thawed

Olive oil spray, for coating the dough

1. In a baking pan, combine the onion, garlic, carrot, and olive oil. 2.Air fry at 200ºC for 2 to 4 minutes, or until the vegetables are crisp-tender. 3.Transfer to a bowl. 4.Stir in the peas and soft white cheese to the vegetable mixture. Let cool while you prepare the dough. 5.Lay one sheet of filo on a work surface and lightly spray with olive oil spray. 6.Top with another sheet of filo. Repeat with the remaining 4 filo sheets; you'll have 3 stacks with 2 layers each. 7.Cut each stack lengthwise into 4 strips (12 strips total). Place a scant 2 teaspoons of the filling near the bottom of each strip. 8.Bring one corner up over the filling to make a triangle; continue folding the triangles over, as you would fold a flag. 9.Seal the edge with a bit of water. Repeat with the remaining strips and filling. 10.Air fry the triangles, in 2 batches, for 4 to 7 minutes, or until golden brown. Serve.

# Meatball Subs

**Prep time: 15 minutes | Cook time: 19 minutes | Serves 6**

Oil, for spraying

450 g 15% fat minced beef

120 ml Italian breadcrumbs (mixed breadcrumbs, Italian seasoning and salt)

1 tablespoon dried minced onion

1 tablespoon minced garlic

1 large egg

1 teaspoon salt

1 teaspoon freshly ground black pepper

6 sub rolls

1 (510 g) jar marinara sauce

350 ml shredded Mozzarella cheese

1. Line the air fryer basket with parchment and spray lightly with oil. 2. In a large bowl, mix together the ground beef, bread crumbs, onion, garlic, egg, salt, and black pepper. Roll the mixture into 18 meatballs. 3. Place the meatballs in the prepared basket. 4. Air fry at 390°F (199°C) for 15 minutes. 5. Place 3 meatballs in each hoagie roll. Top with marinara and Mozzarella cheese. 6. Place the loaded rolls in the air fryer and cook for 3 to 4 minutes, or until the cheese is melted. You may need to work in batches, depending on the size of your air fryer. Serve immediately.

# Pork Burgers with Red Cabbage Salad

**Prep time: 20 minutes | Cook time: 7 to 9 minutes | Serves 4**

120 ml Greek yoghurt

2 tablespoons low-salt mustard, divided

1 tablespoon lemon juice

60 g sliced red cabbage

60 g grated carrots

450 g lean finely chopped pork

½ teaspoon paprika

235 g mixed salad leaves

2 small tomatoes, sliced

8 small low-salt wholemeal sandwich buns, cut in half

1. In a small bowl, combine the yoghurt, 1 tablespoon mustard, lemon juice, cabbage, and carrots; mix and refrigerate. 2.In a medium bowl, combine the pork, remaining 1 tablespoon mustard, and paprika. Form into 8 small patties. Put the sliders into the air fryer basket. 3.Air fry at 200°C for 7 to 9 minutes, or until the sliders register 74°C as tested with a meat thermometer. 4.Assemble the burgers by placing some of the lettuce greens on a bun bottom. 5.Top with a tomato slice, the burgers, and the cabbage mixture. 6.Add the bun top and serve immediately.

# Chapter 3 Fast and Easy Everyday Favourites

# Chapter 3 Fast and Easy Everyday Favourites

## Easy Devils on Horseback

**Prep time: 5 minutes | Cook time: 7 minutes | Serves 12**

| | |
|---|---|
| 24 small pitted prunes (128 g) | 8 slices centre-cut bacon, cut crosswise into thirds |
| 60 g crumbled blue cheese, divided | |

1. Preheat the air fryer to 200ºC. 2.Halve the prunes lengthwise, but don't cut them all the way through. 3.Place ½ teaspoon of cheese in the centre of each prune. 4.Wrap a piece of bacon around each prune and secure the bacon with a toothpick. 5.Working in batches, arrange a single layer of the prunes in the air fryer basket. 6.Air fry for about 7 minutes, flipping halfway, until the bacon is cooked through and crisp. 7.Let cool slightly and serve warm.

## Beery and Crunchy Onion Rings

**Prep time: 10 minutes | Cook time: 16 minutes | Serves 2 to 4**

| | |
|---|---|
| 80 g plain flour | 180 ml beer |
| 1 teaspoon paprika | 175 g breadcrumbs |
| ½ teaspoon bicarbonate of soda | 1 tablespoons olive oil |
| 1 teaspoon salt | 1 large Vidalia or sweet onion, peeled and sliced into ½-inch rings |
| ½ teaspoon freshly ground black pepper | |
| 1 egg, beaten | Cooking spray |

1.Preheat the air fryer to 180ºC. 2.Spritz the air fryer basket with cooking spray. 3.Combine the flour, paprika, bicarbonate of soda, salt, and ground black pepper in a bowl. Stir to mix well. 4.Combine the egg and beer in a separate bowl. Stir to mix well. 5.Make a well in the centre of the flour mixture, then pour the egg mixture in the well. Stir to mix everything well. 6.Pour the breadcrumbs and olive oil in a shallow plate. Stir to mix well. 7.Dredge the onion rings gently into the flour and egg mixture, then shake the excess off and put into the plate of breadcrumbs. Flip to coat both sides well. 8.Arrange the onion rings in the preheated air fryer. 9.Air fry in batches for 16 minutes or until golden brown and crunchy. 10.Flip the rings and put the bottom rings to the top halfway through. 11.Serve immediately.

## Easy Roasted Asparagus

**Prep time: 5 minutes | Cook time: 6 minutes | Serves 4**

| | |
|---|---|
| 450 g asparagus, trimmed and halved crosswise | Salt and pepper, to taste |
| | Lemon wedges, for serving |
| 1 teaspoon extra-virgin olive oil | |

1. Preheat the air fryer to 200ºC. 2.Toss the asparagus with the oil, ⅛ teaspoon salt, and ⅛ teaspoon pepper in bowl. Transfer to air fryer basket. 3.Place the basket in air fryer and roast for 6 to 8 minutes, or until tender and bright green, tossing halfway through cooking. 4.Season with salt and pepper and serve with lemon wedges.

## Scalloped Veggie Mix

**Prep time: 10 minutes | Cook time: 15 minutes | Serves 4**

| | |
|---|---|
| 1 Yukon Gold or other small white potato, thinly sliced | 60 g minced onion |
| | 3 garlic cloves, minced |
| 1 small sweet potato, peeled and thinly sliced | 180 ml 2 percent milk |
| | 2 tablespoons cornflour |
| 1 medium carrot, thinly sliced | ½ teaspoon dried thyme |

1. Preheat the air fryer to 190ºC. 2.In a baking tray, layer the potato, sweet potato, carrot, onion, and garlic. 3.In a small bowl, whisk the milk, cornflour, and thyme until blended. 4.Pour the milk mixture evenly over the vegetables in the pan. Bake for 15 minutes. 5.Check the casserole—it should be golden brown on top, and the vegetables should be tender. 6.Serve immediately.

## Rosemary and Orange Roasted Chickpeas

**Prep time: 5 minutes | Cook time: 10 to 12 minutes | Makes 1 L**

| | |
|---|---|
| 1 kg cooked chickpeas | 1 teaspoon paprika |
| 2 tablespoons vegetable oil | Zest of 1 orange |
| 1 teaspoon rock salt | 1 tablespoon chopped fresh |
| 1 teaspoon cumin | rosemary |

1. Preheat the air fryer to 200ºC. 2.Make sure the chickpeas are completely dry prior to roasting. In a medium bowl, toss the chickpeas with oil, salt, cumin, and paprika. 3.Working in batches, spread the chickpeas in a single layer in the air fryer basket. 4.Air fry for 10 to 12 minutes until crisp, shaking once halfway through. 5.Return the warm chickpeas to the bowl and toss with the orange zest and rosemary. 6.Allow to cool completely. Serve.

## Herb-Roasted Veggies

**Prep time: 10 minutes | Cook time: 14 to 18 minutes | Serves 4**

| | |
|---|---|
| 1 red pepper, sliced | 80 g diced red onion |
| 1 (230 g) package sliced | 3 garlic cloves, sliced |
| mushrooms | 1 teaspoon olive oil |
| 235 g green beans, cut into | ½ teaspoon dried basil |
| 2-inch pieces | ½ teaspoon dried tarragon |

1. Preheat the air fryer to 180ºC. 2.In a medium bowl, mix the red pepper, mushrooms, green beans, red onion, and garlic. 3.Drizzle with the olive oil. Toss to coat. 4.Add the herbs and toss again. Place the vegetables in the air fryer basket. 5.Roast for 14 to 18 minutes, or until tender. 6.Serve immediately.

## Simple and Easy Croutons

**Prep time: 5 minutes | Cook time: 8 minutes | Serves 4**

| | |
|---|---|
| 2 sliced bread | Hot soup, for serving |
| 1 tablespoon olive oil | |

1. Preheat the air fryer to 200ºC. 2.Cut the slices of bread into medium-size chunks. 3.Brush the air fryer basket with the oil. 4.Place the chunks inside and air fry for at least 8 minutes. 5.Serve with hot soup.

## Air Fried Butternut Squash with Chopped Hazelnuts

**Prep time: 10 minutes | Cook time: 20 minutes | Makes 700 ml**

| | |
|---|---|
| 2 tablespoons whole hazelnuts | ¼ teaspoon freshly ground |
| 700 g butternut squash, peeled, | black pepper |
| deseeded, and cubed | 2 teaspoons olive oil |
| ¼ teaspoon rock salt | Cooking spray |

1. Preheat the air fryer to 150ºC. 2.Spritz the air fryer basket with cooking spray. 3.Arrange the hazelnuts in the preheated air fryer. Air fry for 3 minutes or until soft. 4.Chopped the hazelnuts roughly and transfer to a small bowl. Set aside. 5.Set the air fryer temperature to 180ºC. 6.Spritz with cooking spray. Put the butternut squash in a large bowl, then sprinkle with salt and pepper and drizzle with olive oil. 7.Toss to coat well. Transfer the squash in the air fryer. Air fry for 20 minutes or until the squash is soft. 8.Shake the basket halfway through the frying time. 9.When the frying is complete, transfer the squash onto a plate and sprinkle with chopped hazelnuts before serving.

## Purple Potato Chips with Rosemary

**Prep time: 10 minutes | Cook time: 9 to 14 minutes | Serves 6**

| | |
|---|---|
| 235 ml Greek yoghurt | miniature potatoes |
| 2 chipotle chillies, minced | 1 teaspoon olive oil |
| 2 tablespoons adobo or chipotle | 2 teaspoons minced fresh |
| sauce | rosemary leaves |
| 1 teaspoon paprika | ⅛ teaspoon cayenne pepper |
| 1 tablespoon lemon juice | ¼ teaspoon coarse sea salt |
| 10 purple fingerling or | |

1. Preheat the air fryer to 200ºC. 2.In a medium bowl, combine the yoghurt, minced chillies, adobo sauce, paprika, and lemon juice. Mix well and refrigerate. 3.Wash the potatoes and dry them with paper towels. 4.Slice the potatoes lengthwise, as thinly as possible. You can use a mandoline, a vegetable peeler, or a very sharp knife. 5.Combine the potato slices in a medium bowl and drizzle with the olive oil; toss to coat. 6.Air fry the chips, in batches, in the air fryer basket, for 9 to 14 minutes. 7.Use tongs to gently rearrange the chips halfway during cooking time. 8.Sprinkle the chips with the rosemary, cayenne pepper, and sea salt. 9.Serve with the chipotle sauce for dipping.

## Cheesy Potato Patties

**Prep time: 5 minutes | Cook time: 10 minutes | Serves 8**

900 g white potatoes
120 g finely chopped spring onions
½ teaspoon freshly ground black pepper, or more to taste
1 tablespoon fine sea salt
½ teaspoon hot paprika
475 g shredded Colby or Monterey Jack cheese
60 ml rapeseed oil
235 g crushed crackers

1. Preheat the air fryer to 180ºC. Boil the potatoes until soft. 2.Dry them off and peel them before mashing thoroughly, leaving no lumps. 3.Combine the mashed potatoes with spring onions, pepper, salt, paprika, and cheese. 4.Mould the mixture into balls with your hands and press with your palm to flatten them into patties. 5.In a shallow dish, combine the rapeseed oil and crushed crackers. 6.Coat the patties in the crumb mixture. 7.Bake the patties for about 10 minutes, in multiple batches if necessary. 8.Serve hot.

## Air Fried Courgette Sticks

**Prep time: 5 minutes | Cook time: 20 minutes | Serves 4**

1 medium courgette, cut into 48 sticks
30 g seasoned breadcrumbs
1 tablespoon melted margarine
Cooking spray

1. Preheat the air fryer to 180ºC. Spritz the air fryer basket with cooking spray and set aside. In 2 different shallow bowls, add the seasoned breadcrumbs and the margarine. One by one, dredge the courgette sticks into the margarine, then roll in the breadcrumbs to coat evenly. Arrange the crusted sticks on a plate. Place the courgette sticks in the prepared air fryer basket. Work in two batches to avoid overcrowding. Air fry for 10 minutes, or until golden brown and crispy. Shake the basket halfway through to cook evenly. When the cooking time is over, transfer the fries to a wire rack. Rest for 5 minutes and serve warm.

## Buttery Sweet Potatoes

**Prep time: 5 minutes | Cook time: 10 minutes | Serves 4**

2 tablespoons melted butter
1 tablespoon light brown sugar
2 sweet potatoes, peeled and cut
into ½-inch cubes
Cooking spray

1. Preheat the air fryer to 200ºC. 2.Line the air fryer basket with parchment paper. In a medium bowl, stir together the melted butter and brown sugar until blended. 3.Toss the sweet potatoes in the butter mixture until coated. Place the sweet potatoes on the parchment and spritz with oil. 4.Air fry for 5 minutes. Shake the basket, spritz the sweet potatoes with oil, and air fry for 5 minutes more until they're soft enough to cut with a fork. 5.Serve immediately.

## Spinach and Carrot Balls

**Prep time: 10 minutes | Cook time: 10 minutes | Serves 4**

2 slices toasted bread
1 carrot, peeled and grated
1 package fresh spinach, blanched and chopped
½ onion, chopped
1 egg, beaten
½ teaspoon garlic powder
1 teaspoon minced garlic
1 teaspoon salt
½ teaspoon black pepper
1 tablespoon Engevita yeast flakes
1 tablespoon flour

1. Preheat the air fryer to 200ºC. 2.In a food processor, pulse the toasted bread to form breadcrumbs. 3.Transfer into a shallow dish or bowl. In a bowl, mix together all the other ingredients. 4.Use your hands to shape the mixture into small-sized balls. 5.Roll the balls in the breadcrumbs, ensuring to cover them well. 6.Put in the air fryer basket and air fry for 10 minutes. 7.Serve immediately.

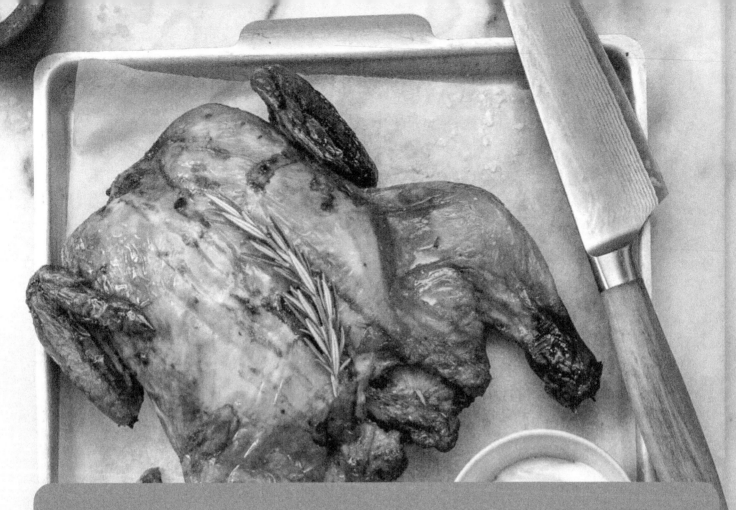

# Chapter 4 Poultry

# Chapter 4 Poultry

## Buttermilk-Fried Drumsticks

**Prep time: 10 minutes | Cook time: 25 minutes | Serves 2**

| | |
|---|---|
| 1 egg | 1 teaspoon salt |
| 120 g buttermilk | ¼ teaspoon ground black |
| 45 g self-rising flour | pepper (to mix into coating) |
| 45 g seasoned panko bread | 4 chicken drumsticks, skin on |
| crumbs | Oil for misting or cooking spray |

1. Beat together egg and buttermilk in shallow dish. 2. In a second shallow dish, combine the flour, panko crumbs, salt, and pepper. 3. Sprinkle chicken legs with additional salt and pepper to taste. 4. Dip legs in buttermilk mixture, then roll in panko mixture, pressing in crumbs to make coating stick. Mist with oil or cooking spray. 5. Spray the air fryer basket with cooking spray. 6. Cook drumsticks at 180ºC for 10 minutes. Turn pieces over and cook an additional 10 minutes. 7. Turn pieces to check for browning. If you have any white spots that haven't begun to brown, spritz them with oil or cooking spray. Continue cooking for 5 more minutes or until crust is golden brown and juices run clear. Larger, meatier drumsticks will take longer to cook than small ones.

## Curried Orange Honey Chicken

**Prep time: 10 minutes | Cook time: 16 to 19 minutes | Serves 4**

| | |
|---|---|
| 340 g boneless, skinless chicken | 60 ml chicken stock |
| thighs, cut into 1-inch pieces | 2 tablespoons honey |
| 1 yellow bell pepper, cut into | 60 ml orange juice |
| 1½-inch pieces | 1 tablespoon cornflour |
| 1 small red onion, sliced | 2 to 3 teaspoons curry powder |
| Olive oil for misting | |

1. Preheat the air fryer to 190ºC. 2. Put the chicken thighs, pepper, and red onion in the air fryer basket and mist with olive oil. 3. Roast for 12 to 14 minutes or until the chicken is cooked to 76ºC, shaking the basket halfway through cooking time. 4. Remove the chicken and vegetables from the air fryer basket and set aside. 5. In a metal bowl, combine the stock, honey, orange juice, cornflour, and curry powder, and mix well. Add the chicken and vegetables, stir, and put the bowl in the basket. 6. Return the basket to the air fryer and roast for 2 minutes. Remove and stir, then roast for 2 to 3 minutes or until the sauce is thickened and bubbly. 7. Serve warm.

## Chicken and Gruyère Cordon Bleu

**Prep time: 15 minutes | Cook time: 15 minutes | Serves 4**

| | |
|---|---|
| 4 chicken breast filets | Freshly ground black pepper, to |
| 75 g chopped ham | taste |
| 75 g grated Swiss cheese, or | ½ teaspoon dried marjoram |
| Gruyère cheese | 1 egg |
| 15 g all-purpose flour | 60 g panko bread crumbs |
| Pinch salt | Olive oil spray |

1. Put the chicken breast filets on a work surface and gently press them with the palm of your hand to make them a bit thinner. Don't tear the meat. 2. In a small bowl, combine the ham and cheese. Divide this mixture among the chicken filets. Wrap the chicken around the filling to enclose it, using toothpicks to hold the chicken together. 3. In a shallow bowl, stir together the flour, salt, pepper, and marjoram. 4. In another bowl, beat the egg. 5. Spread the panko on a plate. 6. Dip the chicken in the flour mixture, in the egg, and in the panko to coat thoroughly. Press the crumbs into the chicken so they stick well. 7. Insert the crisper plate into the basket and the basket into the unit. Preheat the unit by selecting BAKE, setting the temperature to 190ºC, and setting the time to 3 minutes. Select START/STOP to begin. 8. Once the unit is preheated, spray the crisper plate with olive oil. Place the chicken into the basket and spray it with olive oil. 9. Select BAKE, set the temperature to 190ºC, and set the time to 15 minutes. Select START/STOP to begin. 10. When the cooking is complete, the chicken should be cooked through and a food thermometer inserted into the chicken should register 76ºC. Carefully remove the toothpicks and serve.

## Indian Fennel Chicken

**Prep time: 30 minutes | Cook time: 15 minutes | Serves 4**

| | |
|---|---|
| 450 g boneless, skinless chicken thighs, cut crosswise into thirds | 1 teaspoon ground fennel |
| 1 yellow onion, cut into 1½-inch-thick slices | 1 teaspoon garam masala |
| 1 teaspoon ground turmeric | |
| 1 tablespoon coconut oil, melted | 1 teaspoon kosher salt |
| ½ to 1 teaspoon cayenne pepper | |
| 2 teaspoons minced fresh ginger | Vegetable oil spray |
| 2 teaspoons minced garlic | 2 teaspoons fresh lemon juice |
| 1 teaspoon smoked paprika | 5 g chopped fresh coriander or parsley |

1. Use a fork to pierce the chicken all over to allow the marinade to penetrate better. 2. In a large bowl, combine the onion, coconut oil, ginger, garlic, paprika, fennel, garam masala, turmeric, salt, and cayenne. Add the chicken, toss to combine, and marinate at room temperature for 30 minutes, or cover and refrigerate for up to 24 hours. 3. Place the chicken and onion in the air fryer basket. (Discard remaining marinade.) Spray with some vegetable oil spray. Set the air fryer to 180ºC for 15 minutes. Halfway through the cooking time, remove the basket, spray the chicken and onion with more vegetable oil spray, and toss gently to coat. At the end of the cooking time, use a meat thermometer to ensure the chicken has reached an internal temperature of 76ºC. 4. Transfer the chicken and onion to a serving platter. Sprinkle with the lemon juice and coriander and serve.

## Chicken Patties

**Prep time: 15 minutes | Cook time: 12 minutes | Serves 4**

| | |
|---|---|
| 450 g chicken thigh mince | ½ teaspoon garlic powder |
| 110 g shredded Mozzarella cheese | ¼ teaspoon onion powder |
| 1 large egg | |
| 1 teaspoon dried parsley | 60 g pork rinds, finely ground |

1. In a large bowl, mix chicken mince, Mozzarella, parsley, garlic powder, and onion powder. Form into four patties. 2. Place patties in the freezer for 15 to 20 minutes until they begin to firm up. 3. Whisk egg in a medium bowl. Place the ground pork rinds into a large bowl. 4. Dip each chicken patty into the egg and then press into pork rinds to fully coat. Place patties into the air fryer basket. 5. Adjust the temperature to 180ºC and air fry for 12 minutes. 6. Patties will be firm and cooked to an internal temperature of 76ºC when done. Serve immediately.

## Air Fried Chicken Wings with Buffalo Sauce

**Prep time: 10 minutes | Cook time: 20 minutes | Serves 6**

| | |
|---|---|
| 16 chicken drumettes (party wings) | 1 teaspoon garlic powder |
| Ground black pepper, to taste | |
| Chicken seasoning or rub, to taste | 60 ml buffalo wings sauce |
| Cooking spray | |

1. Preheat the air fryer to 200ºC. Spritz the air fryer basket with cooking spray. 2. Rub the chicken wings with chicken seasoning, garlic powder, and ground black pepper on a clean work surface. 3. Arrange the chicken wings in the preheated air fryer. Spritz with cooking spray. Air fry for 10 minutes or until lightly browned. Shake the basket halfway through. 4. Transfer the chicken wings in a large bowl, then pour in the buffalo wings sauce and toss to coat well. 5. Put the wings back to the air fryer and cook for an additional 7 minutes. 6. Serve immediately.

## Tex-Mex Chicken Roll-Ups

**Prep time: 10 minutes | Cook time: 14 to 17 minutes | Serves 8**

| | |
|---|---|
| 900 g boneless, skinless chicken breasts or thighs | black pepper, to taste |
| 170 g Monterey Jack cheese, shredded | |
| 1 teaspoon chili powder | |
| ½ teaspoon smoked paprika | 115 g canned diced green chilies |
| ½ teaspoon ground cumin | |
| Sea salt and freshly ground | Avocado oil spray |

1. Place the chicken in a large zip-top bag or between two pieces of plastic wrap. Using a meat mallet or heavy skillet, pound the chicken until it is about ¼ inch thick. 2. In a small bowl, combine the chili powder, smoked paprika, cumin, and salt and pepper to taste. Sprinkle both sides of the chicken with the seasonings. 3. Sprinkle the chicken with the Monterey Jack cheese, then the diced green chilies. 4. Roll up each piece of chicken from the long side, tucking in the ends as you go. Secure the roll-up with a toothpick. 5. Set the air fryer to 180ºC. . Spray the outside of the chicken with avocado oil. Place the chicken in a single layer in the basket, working in batches if necessary, and roast for 7 minutes. Flip and cook for another 7 to 10 minutes, until an instant-read thermometer reads 70ºC. 6. Remove the chicken from the air fryer and allow it to rest for about 5 minutes before serving.

## Gochujang Chicken Wings

### Prep time: 15 minutes | Cook time: 25 minutes | Serves 4

Wings:
900 g chicken wings
1 teaspoon kosher salt
1 teaspoon black pepper or gochugaru (Korean red pepper)
Sauce:
2 tablespoons gochujang (Korean chili paste)
1 tablespoon mayonnaise
1 tablespoon toasted sesame oil
1 tablespoon minced fresh ginger
1 tablespoon minced garlic
1 teaspoon sugar
1 teaspoon agave nectar or honey
For Serving
1 teaspoon sesame seeds
25 g chopped spring onions

1. For the wings: Season the wings with the salt and pepper and place in the air fryer basket. Set the air fryer to 200°C for 20 minutes, turning the wings halfway through the cooking time. 2. Meanwhile, for the sauce: In a small bowl, combine the gochujang, mayonnaise, sesame oil, ginger, garlic, sugar, and agave; set aside. 3. As you near the 20-minute mark, use a meat thermometer to check the meat. When the wings reach 70°C, transfer them to a large bowl. Pour about half the sauce on the wings; toss to coat (serve the remaining sauce as a dip). 4. Return the wings to the air fryer basket and cook for 5 minutes, until the sauce has glazed. 5. Transfer the wings to a serving platter. Sprinkle with the sesame seeds and spring onions. Serve with the reserved sauce on the side for dipping.

## Teriyaki Chicken Thighs with Lemony Snow Peas

### Prep time: 30 minutes | Cook time: 34 minutes | Serves 4

60 ml chicken broth
½ teaspoon grated fresh ginger
⅛ teaspoon red pepper flakes
1½ tablespoons soy sauce
4 (140 g) bone-in chicken thighs, trimmed
1 tablespoon mirin
½ teaspoon cornflour
1 tablespoon sugar
170 g mangetout, strings removed
⅛ teaspoon lemon zest
1 garlic clove, minced
¼ teaspoon salt
Ground black pepper, to taste
½ teaspoon lemon juice

1. Combine the broth, ginger, pepper flakes, and soy sauce in a large bowl. Stir to mix well. 2. Pierce 10 to 15 holes into the chicken skin. Put the chicken in the broth mixture and toss to coat well. Let sit for 10 minutes to marinate. 3. Preheat the air fryer to 206°C. 4. Transfer the marinated chicken on a plate and pat dry with paper towels. 5. Scoop 2 tablespoons of marinade in a microwave-safe bowl and combine with mirin, cornflour and sugar. Stir to mix well. Microwave for 1 minute or until frothy and has a thick consistency. Set aside. 6. Arrange the chicken in the preheated air fryer, skin side up, and air fry for 25 minutes or until the internal temperature of the chicken reaches at least 76°C. Gently turn the chicken over halfway through. 7. When the frying is complete, brush the chicken skin with marinade mixture. Air fryer the chicken for 5 more minutes or until glazed. 8. Remove the chicken from the air fryer and reserve ½ teaspoon of chicken fat remains in the air fryer. Allow the chicken to cool for 10 minutes. 9. Meanwhile, combine the reserved chicken fat, snow peas, lemon zest, garlic, salt, and ground black pepper in a small bowl. Toss to coat well. 10. Transfer the snow peas in the air fryer and air fry for 3 minutes or until soft. Remove the peas from the air fryer and toss with lemon juice. 11. Serve the chicken with lemony snow peas.

## Fiesta Chicken Plate

### Prep time: 15 minutes | Cook time: 12 to 15 minutes | Serves 4

450 g boneless, skinless chicken breasts (2 large breasts)
2 tablespoons lime juice
1 teaspoon cumin
½ teaspoon salt
40 g grated Pepper Jack cheese
1 (455 g) can refried beans
130 g salsa
30 g shredded lettuce
1 medium tomato, chopped
2 avocados, peeled and sliced
1 small onion, sliced into thin rings
Sour cream
Tortilla chips (optional)

1. Split each chicken breast in half lengthwise. 2. Mix lime juice, cumin, and salt together and brush on all surfaces of chicken breasts. 3. Place in air fryer basket and air fry at 200°C for 12 to 15 minutes, until well done. 4. Divide the cheese evenly over chicken breasts and cook for an additional minute to melt cheese. 5. While chicken is cooking, heat refried beans on stovetop or in microwave. 6. When ready to serve, divide beans among 4 plates. Place chicken breasts on top of beans and spoon salsa over. Arrange the lettuce, tomatoes, and avocados artfully on each plate and scatter with the onion rings. 7. Pass sour cream at the table and serve with tortilla chips if desired.

# Brazilian Tempero Baiano Chicken Drumsticks

**Prep time: 30 minutes | Cook time: 20 minutes | Serves 4**

| | |
|---|---|
| 1 teaspoon cumin seeds | ½ teaspoon black peppercorns |
| 1 teaspoon dried oregano | ½ teaspoon cayenne pepper |
| 1 teaspoon dried parsley | 60 ml fresh lime juice |
| 1 teaspoon ground turmeric | 2 tablespoons olive oil |
| ½ teaspoon coriander seeds | 680 g chicken drumsticks |
| 1 teaspoon kosher salt | |

1. In a clean coffee grinder or spice mill, combine the cumin, oregano, parsley, turmeric, coriander seeds, salt, peppercorns, and cayenne. Process until finely ground. 2. In a small bowl, combine the ground spices with the lime juice and oil. Place the chicken in a resealable plastic bag. Add the marinade, seal, and massage until the chicken is well coated. Marinate at room temperature for 30 minutes or in the refrigerator for up to 24 hours. 3. When you are ready to cook, place the drumsticks skin side up in the air fryer basket. Set the air fryer to 200°C for 20 to 25 minutes, turning the legs halfway through the cooking time. Use a meat thermometer to ensure that the chicken has reached an internal temperature of 76°C. 4. Serve with plenty of napkins.

# Chicken Manchurian

**Prep time: 10 minutes | Cook time: 20 minutes | Serves 2**

| | |
|---|---|
| 450 g boneless, skinless chicken breasts, cut into 1-inch pieces | 2 teaspoons vegetable oil |
| 60 g ketchup | 1 teaspoon hot sauce, such as Tabasco |
| 1 tablespoon tomato-based chili sauce, such as Heinz | ½ teaspoon garlic powder |
| 1 tablespoon soy sauce | ¼ teaspoon cayenne pepper |
| 1 tablespoon rice vinegar | 2 spring onions, thinly sliced |
| | Cooked white rice, for serving |

1. Preheat the air fryer to 180°C. 2. In a bowl, combine the chicken, ketchup, chili sauce, soy sauce, vinegar, oil, hot sauce, garlic powder, cayenne, and three-quarters of the spring onions and toss until evenly coated. 3. Scrape the chicken and sauce into a metal cake pan and place the pan in the air fryer. Bake until the chicken is cooked through and the sauce is reduced to a thick glaze, about 20 minutes, flipping the chicken pieces halfway through. 4. Remove the pan from the air fryer. Spoon the chicken and sauce over rice and top with the remaining spring onions. Serve immediately.

# Buttermilk Breaded Chicken

**Prep time: 7 minutes | Cook time: 20 to 25 minutes | Serves 4**

| | |
|---|---|
| 125 g all-purpose flour | 2 tablespoons extra-virgin olive oil |
| 2 teaspoons paprika | |
| Pinch salt | 185 g bread crumbs |
| Freshly ground black pepper, to taste | 6 chicken pieces, drumsticks, breasts, and thighs, patted dry |
| 80 ml buttermilk | Cooking oil spray |
| 2 eggs | |

1. In a shallow bowl, stir together the flour, paprika, salt, and pepper. 2. In another bowl, beat the buttermilk and eggs until smooth. 3. In a third bowl, stir together the olive oil and bread crumbs until mixed. 4. Dredge the chicken in the flour, dip in the eggs to coat, and finally press into the bread crumbs, patting the crumbs firmly onto the chicken skin. 5. Insert the crisper plate into the basket and the basket into the unit. Preheat the unit by selecting AIR FRY, setting the temperature to 190°C, and setting the time to 3 minutes. Select START/STOP to begin. 6. Once the unit is preheated, spray the crisper plate with cooking oil. Place the chicken into the basket. 7. Select AIR FRY, set the temperature to 190°C, and set the time to 25 minutes. Select START/STOP to begin. 8. After 10 minutes, flip the chicken. Resume cooking. After 10 minutes more, check the chicken. If a food thermometer inserted into the chicken registers 76°C and the chicken is brown and crisp, it is done. Otherwise, resume cooking for up to 5 minutes longer. 9. When the cooking is complete, let cool for 5 minutes, then serve.

# Almond-Crusted Chicken

**Prep time: 15 minutes | Cook time: 25 minutes | Serves 4**

| | |
|---|---|
| 20 g slivered almonds | 2 tablespoons full-fat mayonnaise |
| 2 (170 g) boneless, skinless chicken breasts | 1 tablespoon Dijon mustard |

1. Pulse the almonds in a food processor or chop until finely chopped. Place almonds evenly on a plate and set aside. 2. Completely slice each chicken breast in half lengthwise. 3. Mix the mayonnaise and mustard in a small bowl and then coat chicken with the mixture. 4. Lay each piece of chicken in the chopped almonds to fully coat. Carefully move the pieces into the air fryer basket. 5. Adjust the temperature to 180°C and air fry for 25 minutes. 6. Chicken will be done when it has reached an internal temperature of 76°C or more. Serve warm.

# Ham Chicken with Cheese

**Prep time: 15 minutes | Cook time: 25 minutes |**
**Serves 4**

| | |
|---|---|
| 55 g unsalted butter, softened | 60 ml water |
| 115 g cream cheese, softened | 280 g shredded cooked chicken |
| 1½ teaspoons Dijon mustard | 115 g ham, chopped |
| 2 tablespoons white wine vinegar | 115 g sliced Swiss or Provolone cheese |

1. Preheat the air fryer to 190ºC. Lightly coat a casserole dish that will fit in the air fryer, such as an 8-inch round pan, with olive oil and set aside. 2. In a large bowl and using an electric mixer, combine the butter, cream cheese, Dijon mustard, and vinegar. With the motor running at low speed, slowly add the water and beat until smooth. Set aside. 3. Arrange an even layer of chicken in the bottom of the prepared pan, followed by the ham. Spread the butter and cream cheese mixture on top of the ham, followed by the cheese slices on the top layer. Air fry for 20 to 25 minutes until warmed through and the cheese has browned.

# Mediterranean Stuffed Chicken Breasts

**Prep time: 5 minutes | Cook time: 20 to 25 minutes |**
**Serves 4**

| | |
|---|---|
| 4 small boneless, skinless chicken breast halves (about 680 g) | Zest of ½ lemon |
| | 1 teaspoon minced fresh rosemary or ½ teaspoon ground dried rosemary |
| Salt and freshly ground black pepper, to taste | 25 g almond meal |
| 115 g goat cheese | 60 ml balsamic vinegar |
| 6 pitted Kalamata olives, coarsely chopped | 6 tablespoons unsalted butter |

1. Preheat the air fryer to 180ºC. 2. With a boning knife, cut a wide pocket into the thickest part of each chicken breast half, taking care not to cut all the way through. Season the chicken evenly on both sides with salt and freshly ground black pepper. 3. In a small bowl, mix the cheese, olives, lemon zest, and rosemary. Stuff the pockets with the cheese mixture and secure with toothpicks. 4. Place the almond meal in a shallow bowl and dredge the chicken, shaking off the excess. Coat lightly with olive oil spray. 5. Working in batches if necessary, arrange the chicken breasts in a single layer in the air fryer basket. Pausing halfway through the cooking time to flip the chicken, air fry for 20 to 25 minutes, until a thermometer inserted into the thickest part registers 76ºC. 6. While the chicken is baking, prepare the sauce. In a small pan over medium heat, simmer the balsamic vinegar until thick and syrupy, about 5 minutes. Set aside until the chicken is done. When ready to serve, warm the sauce over medium heat and whisk in the butter, 1 tablespoon at a time, until melted and smooth. Season to taste with salt and pepper. 7. Serve the chicken breasts with the sauce drizzled on top.

# Pecan-Crusted Chicken Tenders

**Prep time: 10 minutes | Cook time: 12 minutes |**
**Serves 4**

| | |
|---|---|
| 2 tablespoons mayonnaise | ¼ teaspoon ground black pepper |
| 1 teaspoon Dijon mustard | |
| 455 g boneless, skinless chicken tenders | 75 g chopped roasted pecans, finely ground |
| ½ teaspoon salt | |

1. In a small bowl, whisk mayonnaise and mustard until combined. Brush mixture onto chicken tenders on both sides, then sprinkle tenders with salt and pepper. 2. Place pecans in a medium bowl and press each tender into pecans to coat each side. 3. Place tenders into ungreased air fryer basket in a single layer, working in batches if needed. Adjust the temperature to (190ºC and roast for 12 minutes, turning tenders halfway through cooking. Tenders will be golden brown and have an internal temperature of at least 76ºC when done. Serve warm.

# Crunchy Chicken Tenders

**Prep time: 5 minutes | Cook time: 12 minutes |**
**Serves 4**

| | |
|---|---|
| 1 egg | ½ teaspoon black pepper |
| 60 ml unsweetened almond milk | ½ teaspoon dried thyme |
| | ½ teaspoon dried sage |
| 15 g whole wheat flour | ½ teaspoon garlic powder |
| 15 g whole wheat bread crumbs | 450 g chicken tenderloins |
| ½ teaspoon salt | 1 lemon, quartered |

1. Preheat the air fryer to 184ºC. 2. In a shallow bowl, beat together the egg and almond milk until frothy. 3. In a separate shallow bowl, whisk together the flour, bread crumbs, salt, pepper, thyme, sage, and garlic powder. 4. Dip each chicken tenderloin into the egg mixture, then into the bread crumb mixture, coating the outside with the crumbs. Place the breaded chicken tenderloins into the bottom of the air fryer basket in an even layer, making sure that they don't touch each other. 5. Cook for 6 minutes, then turn and cook for an additional 5 to 6 minutes. Serve with lemon slices.

## Buffalo Crispy Chicken Strips

**Prep time: 15 minutes | Cook time: 13 to 17 minutes per batch | Serves 4**

45 g all-purpose flour

2 eggs

2 tablespoons water

60 g seasoned panko bread crumbs

2 teaspoons granulated garlic

1 teaspoon salt

1 teaspoon freshly ground black

pepper

16 chicken breast strips, or 3 large boneless, skinless chicken breasts, cut into 1-inch strips

Olive oil spray

60 ml Buffalo sauce, plus more as needed

1. Put the flour in a small bowl. 2. In another small bowl, whisk the eggs and the water. 3. In a third bowl, stir together the panko, granulated garlic, salt, and pepper. 4. Dip each chicken strip in the flour, in the egg, and in the panko mixture to coat. Press the crumbs onto the chicken with your fingers. 5. Insert the crisper plate into the basket and the basket into the unit. Preheat the unit by selecting AIR FRY, setting the temperature to 190ºC, and setting the time to 3 minutes. Select START/STOP to begin. 6. Once the unit is preheated, place a parchment paper liner into the basket. Working in batches if needed, place the chicken strips into the basket. Do not stack unless using a wire rack for the second layer. Spray the top of the chicken with olive oil. 7. Select AIR FRY, set the temperature to 190ºC, and set the time to 17 minutes. Select START/STOP to begin. 8. After 10 or 12 minutes, remove the basket, flip the chicken, and spray again with olive oil. Reinsert the basket to resume cooking. 9. When the cooking is complete, the chicken should be golden brown and crispy and a food thermometer inserted into the chicken should register 76ºC. 10. Repeat steps 6, 7, and 8 with any remaining chicken. 11. Transfer the chicken to a large bowl. Drizzle the Buffalo sauce over the top of the cooked chicken, toss to coat, and serve.

## Pork Rind Fried Chicken

**Prep time: 30 minutes | Cook time: 20 minutes | Serves 4**

60 ml buffalo sauce

4 (115 g) boneless, skinless chicken breasts

½ teaspoon paprika

½ teaspoon garlic powder

¼ teaspoon ground black pepper

60 g g plain pork rinds, finely crushed

1. Pour buffalo sauce into a large sealable bowl or bag. Add chicken and toss to coat. Place sealed bowl or bag into refrigerator and let marinate at least 30 minutes up to overnight. 2. Remove chicken from marinade but do not shake excess sauce off chicken. Sprinkle both sides of thighs with paprika, garlic powder, and pepper. 3. Place pork rinds into a large bowl and press each chicken breast into pork rinds to coat evenly on both sides. 4. Place chicken into ungreased air fryer basket. Adjust the temperature to 200ºC and roast for 20 minutes, turning chicken halfway through cooking. Chicken will be golden and have an internal temperature of at least 76ºC when done. Serve warm.

## Chicken Rochambeau

**Prep time: 15 minutes | Cook time: 20 minutes | Serves 4**

1 tablespoon butter

4 chicken tenders, cut in half crosswise

Salt and pepper, to taste

15 g flour

Oil for misting

4 slices ham, ¼- to ⅜-inches thick and large enough to cover an English muffin

2 English muffins, split

Sauce:

2 tablespoons butter

25 g chopped green onions

50 g chopped mushrooms

2 tablespoons flour

240 ml chicken broth

¼ teaspoon garlic powder

1½ teaspoons Worcestershire sauce

1. Place 1 tablespoon of butter in a baking pan and air fry at 200ºC for 2 minutes to melt. 2. Sprinkle chicken tenders with salt and pepper to taste, then roll in the flour. 3. Place chicken in baking pan, turning pieces to coat with melted butter. 4. Air fry at 200ºC for 5 minutes. Turn chicken pieces over, and spray tops lightly with olive oil. Cook 5 minutes longer or until juices run clear. The chicken will not brown. 5. While chicken is cooking, make the sauce: In a medium saucepan, melt the 2 tablespoons of butter. 6. Add onions and mushrooms and sauté until tender, about 3 minutes. 7. Stir in the flour. Gradually add broth, stirring constantly until you have a smooth gravy. 8. Add garlic powder and Worcestershire sauce and simmer on low heat until sauce thickens, about 5 minutes. 9. When chicken is cooked, remove baking pan from air fryer and set aside. 10. Place ham slices directly into air fryer basket and air fry at 200ºC for 5 minutes or until hot and beginning to sizzle a little. Remove and set aside on top of the chicken for now. 11. Place the English muffin halves in air fryer basket and air fry at 200ºC for 1 minute. 12. Open air fryer and place a ham slice on top of each English muffin half. Stack 2 pieces of chicken on top of each ham slice. Air fry for 1 to 2 minutes to heat through. 13. Place each English muffin stack on a serving plate and top with plenty of sauce.

# Cracked-Pepper Chicken Wings

### Prep time: 15 minutes | Cook time: 20 minutes | Serves 4

450 g chicken wings
3 tablespoons vegetable oil
30 g all-purpose flour
½ teaspoon smoked paprika

½ teaspoon garlic powder
½ teaspoon kosher salt
1½ teaspoons freshly cracked black pepper

1. Place the chicken wings in a large bowl. Drizzle the vegetable oil over wings and toss to coat. 2. In a separate bowl, whisk together the flour, paprika, garlic powder, salt, and pepper until combined. 3. Dredge the wings in the flour mixture one at a time, coating them well, and place in the air fryer basket. Set the air fryer to 200°C for 20 minutes, turning the wings halfway through the cooking time, until the breading is browned and crunchy.

# Chicken Breasts with Asparagus, Beans, and Rocket

### Prep time: 20 minutes | Cook time: 25 minutes | Serves 2

160 g canned cannellini beans, rinsed
1½ tablespoons red wine vinegar
1 garlic clove, minced
2 tablespoons extra-virgin olive oil, divided
Salt and ground black pepper, to taste

½ red onion, sliced thinly
230 g asparagus, trimmed and cut into 1-inch lengths
2 (230 g) boneless, skinless chicken breasts, trimmed
¼ teaspoon paprika
½ teaspoon ground coriander
60 g baby rocket, rinsed and drained

1. Preheat the air fryer to 200°C. 2. Warm the beans in microwave for 1 minutes and combine with red wine vinegar, garlic, 1 tablespoon of olive oil, ¼ teaspoon of salt, and ¼ teaspoon of ground black pepper in a bowl. Stir to mix well. 3. Combine the onion with ⅛ teaspoon of salt, ⅛ teaspoon of ground black pepper, and 2 teaspoons of olive oil in a separate bowl. Toss to coat well. 4. Place the onion in the air fryer and air fry for 2 minutes, then add the asparagus and air fry for 8 more minutes or until the asparagus is tender. Shake the basket halfway through. Transfer the onion and asparagus to the bowl with beans. Set aside. 5. Toss the chicken breasts with remaining ingredients, except for the baby rocket, in a large bowl. 6. Put the chicken breasts in the air fryer and air

fry for 14 minutes or until the internal temperature of the chicken reaches at least 76°C. Flip the breasts halfway through. 7. Remove the chicken from the air fryer and serve on an aluminum foil with asparagus, beans, onion, and rocket. Sprinkle with salt and ground black pepper. Toss to serve.

# Cornish Hens with Honey-Lime Glaze

### Prep time: 15 minutes | Cook time: 25 to 30 minutes | Serves 2 to 3

1 small chicken (680 to 900 g)
1 tablespoon honey
1 tablespoon lime juice

1 teaspoon poultry seasoning
Salt and pepper, to taste
Cooking spray

1. To split the chicken into halves, cut through breast bone and down one side of the backbone. 2. Mix the honey, lime juice, and poultry seasoning together and brush or rub onto all sides of the chicken. Season to taste with salt and pepper. 3. Spray the air fryer basket with cooking spray and place hen halves in the basket, skin-side down. 4. Air fry at 170°C for 25 to 30 minutes. Chicken will be done when juices run clear when pierced at leg joint with a fork. Let chicken rest for 5 to 10 minutes before cutting.

# Gold Livers

### Prep time: 10 minutes | Cook time: 20 minutes | Serves 4

2 eggs
2 tablespoons water
45 g flour
120 g panko breadcrumbs
1 teaspoon salt

½ teaspoon ground black pepper
570 g chicken livers
Cooking spray

1. Preheat the air fryer to 200°C. Spritz the air fryer basket with cooking spray. 2. Whisk the eggs with water in a large bowl. Pour the flour in a separate bowl. Pour the panko on a shallow dish and sprinkle with salt and pepper. 3. Dredge the chicken livers in the flour. Shake the excess off, then dunk the livers in the whisked eggs, and then roll the livers over the panko to coat well. 4. Arrange the livers in the preheated air fryer and spritz with cooking spray. Work in batches to avoid overcrowding. 5. Air fry for 10 minutes or until the livers are golden and crispy. Flip the livers halfway through. Repeat with remaining livers. 6. Serve immediately.

# Chapter 5 Fish and Seafood

# Chapter 5 Fish and Seafood

## Cornmeal-Crusted Trout Fingers

**Prep time: 15 minutes | Cook time: 6 minutes |**
**Serves 2**

70 g yellow cornmeal, medium or finely ground (not coarse)
20 g plain flour
1½ teaspoons baking powder
1 teaspoon kosher or coarse sea salt, plus more as needed
½ teaspoon freshly ground black pepper, plus more as needed
⅛ teaspoon cayenne pepper
340 g skinless trout fillets, cut

into strips 1 inch wide and 3 inches long
3 large eggs, lightly beaten
Cooking spray
115 g mayonnaise
2 tablespoons capers, rinsed and finely chopped
1 tablespoon fresh tarragon
1 teaspoon fresh lemon juice, plus lemon wedges, for serving

1. Preheat the air fryer to 200ºC. 2. In a large bowl, whisk together the cornmeal, flour, baking powder, salt, black pepper, and cayenne. Dip the trout strips in the egg, then toss them in the cornmeal mixture until fully coated. Transfer the trout to a rack set over a baking sheet and liberally spray all over with cooking spray. 3. Transfer half the fish to the air fryer and air fry until the fish is cooked through and golden brown, about 6 minutes. Transfer the fish sticks to a plate and repeat with the remaining fish. 4. Meanwhile, in a bowl, whisk together the mayonnaise, capers, tarragon, and lemon juice. Season the tartar sauce with salt and black pepper. 5. Serve the trout fingers hot along with the tartar sauce and lemon wedges.

## Tilapia with Pecans

**Prep time: 20 minutes | Cook time: 16 minutes |**
**Serves 5**

2 tablespoons ground flaxseeds
1 teaspoon paprika
Sea salt and white pepper, to taste
1 teaspoon garlic paste

2 tablespoons extra virgin olive oil
65 g pecans, ground
5 tilapia fillets, sliced into halves

1. Combine the ground flaxseeds, paprika, salt, white pepper, garlic paste, olive oil, and ground pecans in a sealable freezer bag. Add the fish fillets and shake to coat well. 2. Spritz the air fryer basket with cooking spray. Cook in the preheated air fryer at 200ºC for 10 minutes; turn them over and cook for 6 minutes more. Work in batches. 3. Serve with lemon wedges, if desired. Enjoy!

## Easy Scallops

**Prep time: 5 minutes | Cook time: 4 minutes | Serves 2**

12 medium sea scallops, rinsed and patted dry
1 teaspoon fine sea salt
¾ teaspoon ground black

pepper, plus more for garnish
Fresh thyme leaves, for garnish (optional)
Avocado oil spray

1. Preheat the air fryer to 200ºC. Coat the air fryer basket with avocado oil spray. 2. Place the scallops in a medium bowl and spritz with avocado oil spray. Sprinkle the salt and pepper to season. 3. Transfer the seasoned scallops to the air fryer basket, spacing them apart. You may need to work in batches to avoid overcrowding. 4. Air fry for 4 minutes, flipping the scallops halfway through, or until the scallops are firm and reach an internal temperature of just 64ºC on a meat thermometer. 5. Remove from the basket and repeat with the remaining scallops. 6. Sprinkle the pepper and thyme leaves on top for garnish, if desired. Serve immediately.

## Coconut Cream Mackerel

**Prep time: 10 minutes | Cook time: 6 minutes |**
**Serves 4**

900 g mackerel fillet
240 ml coconut cream
1 teaspoon ground coriander

1 teaspoon cumin seeds
1 garlic clove, peeled, chopped

1. Chop the mackerel roughly and sprinkle it with coconut cream, ground coriander, cumin seeds, and garlic. 2. Then put the fish in the air fryer and cook at 200ºC for 6 minutes.

## Tuna Patties with Spicy Sriracha Sauce

**Prep time: 10 minutes | Cook time: 10 minutes | Serves 4**

| | |
|---|---|
| 2 (170 g) cans tuna packed in oil, drained | Pinch of salt and pepper |
| 3 tablespoons almond flour | Spicy Sriracha Sauce: |
| 2 tablespoons mayonnaise | 60 g mayonnaise |
| 1 teaspoon dried dill | 1 tablespoon Sriracha sauce |
| ½ teaspoon onion powder | 1 teaspoon garlic powder |

1. Preheat the air fryer to 190ºC. Line the basket with baking paper. 2. In a large bowl, combine the tuna, almond flour, mayonnaise, dill, and onion powder. Season to taste with salt and freshly ground black pepper. Use a fork to stir, mashing with the back of the fork as necessary, until thoroughly combined. 3. Use an ice cream scoop to form the tuna mixture patties. Place the patties in a single layer on the baking paper in the air fryer basket. Press lightly with the bottom of the scoop to flatten into a circle about ½ inch thick. Pausing halfway through the cooking time to turn the patties, air fry for 10 minutes until lightly browned. 4. To make the Sriracha sauce: In a small bowl, combine the mayonnaise, Sriracha, and garlic powder. Serve the tuna patties topped with the Sriracha sauce.

## Fish Tacos with Jalapeño-Lime Sauce

**Prep time: 25 minutes | Cook time: 7 to 10 minutes | Serves 4**

| | |
|---|---|
| Fish Tacos: | 120 ml sour cream |
| 455 g firm white fish fillets | 1 tablespoon lime juice |
| ¼ teaspoon cumin | ¼ teaspoon grated lime zest |
| ¼ teaspoon coriander | ½ teaspoon minced jalapeño |
| ⅛ teaspoon ground red pepper | (flesh only) |
| 1 tablespoon lime zest | ¼ teaspoon cumin |
| ¼ teaspoon smoked paprika | Napa Cabbage Garnish: |
| 1 teaspoon oil | 90 g shredded Savoy cabbage |
| Cooking spray | 40 g sliced red or green bell |
| 6 to 8 corn or flour tortillas (6-inch size) | pepper |
| | 30 g sliced onion |
| Jalapeño-Lime Sauce: | |

1. Slice the fish fillets into strips approximately ½-inch thick. 2. Put the strips into a sealable plastic bag along with the cumin, coriander, red pepper, lime zest, smoked paprika, and oil. Massage seasonings into the fish until evenly distributed. 3. Spray the air fryer basket with nonstick cooking spray and place seasoned fish inside. 4. Air fry at 200ºC for approximately 5 minutes. Shake basket to distribute fish. Cook an additional 2 to 5 minutes, until fish flakes easily. 5. While the fish is cooking, prepare the Jalapeño-Lime Sauce by mixing the sour cream, lime juice, lime zest, jalapeño, and cumin together to make a smooth sauce. Set aside. 6. Mix the cabbage, bell pepper, and onion together and set aside. 7. To warm refrigerated tortillas, wrap in damp paper towels and microwave for 30 to 60 seconds. 8. To serve, spoon some of fish into a warm tortilla. Add one or two tablespoons Napa Cabbage Garnish and drizzle with Jalapeño-Lime Sauce.

## Mustard-Crusted Fish Fillets

**Prep time: 5 minutes | Cook time: 8 to 11 minutes | Serves 4**

| | |
|---|---|
| 5 teaspoons yellow mustard | ⅛ teaspoon freshly ground |
| 1 tablespoon freshly squeezed lemon juice | black pepper |
| | 1 slice whole-wheat bread, |
| 4 sole fillets, 100 g each | crumbled |
| ½ teaspoon dried thyme | 2 teaspoons olive oi |
| ½ teaspoon dried marjoram | |

1. In a small bowl, mix the mustard and lemon juice. Spread this evenly over the fillets. Place them in the air fryer basket. 2. In another small bowl, mix the thyme, marjoram, pepper, bread crumbs, and olive oil. Mix until combined. 3. Gently but firmly press the spice mixture onto the top of each fish fillet. 4. Bake at 160ºC for 8 to 11 minutes, or until the fish reaches an internal temperature of at least 64ºC on a meat thermometer and the topping is browned and crisp. Serve immediately.

## Crispy Fish Sticks

**Prep time: 15 minutes | Cook time: 10 minutes | Serves 4**

| | |
|---|---|
| 20 g crushed panko breadcrumbs | 1 tablespoon coconut oil |
| | 1 large egg |
| 20 g blanched finely ground almond flour | 455 g cod fillet, cut into ¾-inch strips |
| ½ teaspoon Old Bay seasoning | |

1. Place panko, almond flour, Old Bay seasoning, and coconut oil into a large bowl and mix together. In a medium bowl, whisk egg. 2. Dip each fish stick into the egg and then gently press into the flour mixture, coating as fully and evenly as possible. Place fish sticks into the air fryer basket. 3. Adjust the temperature to 200ºC and air fry for 10 minutes or until golden. 4. Serve immediately.

# Tilapia Almondine

## Prep time: 10 minutes | Cook time: 10 minutes | Serves 2

25 g almond flour or fine dried bread crumbs

2 tablespoons salted butter or ghee, melted

1 teaspoon black pepper

½ teaspoon kosher or coarse sea

salt

60 g mayonnaise

2 tilapia fillets

435 g thinly sliced almonds

Vegetable oil spray

1. In a small bowl, mix together the almond flour, butter, pepper and salt. 2. Spread the mayonnaise on both sides of each fish fillet. Dredge the fillets in the almond flour mixture. Spread the sliced almonds on one side of each fillet, pressing lightly to adhere. 3. Spray the air fryer basket with vegetable oil spray. Place the fish fillets in the basket. Set the air fryer to 160°C for 10 minutes, or until the fish flakes easily with a fork.

# Stuffed Sole Florentine

## Prep time: 10 minutes | Cook time: 25 minutes | Serves 4

40 g pine nuts

2 tablespoons olive oil

90 g chopped tomatoes

170 g bag spinach, coarsely chopped

2 cloves garlic, chopped

Salt and freshly ground black

pepper, to taste

2 tablespoons unsalted butter, divided

4 Sole fillets (about 680 g)

Dash of paprika

½ lemon, sliced into 4 wedges

1. Place the pine nuts in a baking dish that fits in your air fryer. Set the air fryer to 200°C and air fry for 4 minutes until the nuts are lightly browned and fragrant. Remove the baking dish from the air fryer, tip the nuts onto a plate to cool, and continue preheating the air fryer. When the nuts are cool enough to handle, chop them into fine pieces. 2. In the baking dish, combine the oil, tomatoes, spinach, and garlic. Use tongs to toss until thoroughly combined. Air fry for 5 minutes until the tomatoes are softened and the spinach is wilted. 3. Transfer the vegetables to a bowl and stir in the toasted pine nuts. Season to taste with salt and freshly ground black pepper. 4. Place 1 tablespoon of the butter in the bottom of the baking dish. Lower the heat on the air fryer to 180°C. 5. Place the sole on a clean work surface. Sprinkle both sides with salt and black pepper. Divide the vegetable mixture among the sole fillets and carefully roll up, securing with toothpicks. 6. Working in batches if necessary, arrange the fillets seam-side down in the

baking dish along with 1 tablespoon of water. Top the fillets with remaining 1 tablespoon butter and sprinkle with a dash of paprika. 7. Cover loosely with foil and air fry for 10 to 15 minutes until the fish is opaque and flakes easily with a fork. Remove the toothpicks before serving with the lemon wedges.

# Cod with Avocado

## Prep time: 30 minutes | Cook time: 10 minutes | Serves 2

90 g shredded cabbage

60 ml full-fat sour cream

2 tablespoons full-fat mayonnaise

20 g chopped pickled jalapeños

2 (85 g) cod fillets

1 teaspoon chilli powder

1 teaspoon cumin

½ teaspoon paprika

¼ teaspoon garlic powder

1 medium avocado, peeled, pitted, and sliced

½ medium lime

1. In a large bowl, place cabbage, sour cream, mayonnaise, and jalapeños. Mix until fully coated. Let sit for 20 minutes in the refrigerator. 2. Sprinkle cod fillets with chilli powder, cumin, paprika, and garlic powder. Place each fillet into the air fryer basket. 3. Adjust the temperature to 190°C and set the timer for 10 minutes. 4. Flip the fillets halfway through the cooking time. When fully cooked, fish should have an internal temperature of at least 64°C. 5. To serve, divide slaw mixture into two serving bowls, break cod fillets into pieces and spread over the bowls, and top with avocado. Squeeze lime juice over each bowl. Serve immediately.

# Air Fryer Fish Fry

## Prep time: 5 minutes | Cook time: 15 minutes | Serves 4

470 ml low-fat buttermilk

½ teaspoon garlic powder

½ teaspoon onion powder

4 (110 g) sole fillets

35 g plain yellow cornmeal

25 g chickpea flour

¼ teaspoon cayenne pepper

Freshly ground black pepper

1. In a large bowl, combine the buttermilk, garlic powder, and onion powder. 2. Add the sole, turning until well coated, and set aside to marinate for 20 minutes. 3. In a shallow bowl, stir the cornmeal, chickpea flour, cayenne, and pepper together. 4. Dredge the fillets in the meal mixture, turning until well coated. Place in the basket of an air fryer. 5. Set the air fryer to 190°C, close, and cook for 12 minutes.

## Roasted Halibut Steaks with Parsley

### Prep time: 5 minutes | Cook time: 10 minutes | Serves 4

455 g halibut steaks
60 ml vegetable oil
2½ tablespoons Worcester sauce
2 tablespoons honey
2 tablespoons vermouth or white wine vinegar

1 tablespoon freshly squeezed lemon juice
1 tablespoon fresh parsley leaves, coarsely chopped
Salt and pepper, to taste
1 teaspoon dried basil

1. Preheat the air fryer to 200°C. 2. Put all the ingredients in a large mixing dish and gently stir until the fish is coated evenly. 3. Transfer the fish to the air fryer basket and roast for 10 minutes, flipping the fish halfway through, or until the fish reaches an internal temperature of at least 64°C on a meat thermometer. 4. Let the fish cool for 5 minutes and serve.

## Sole and Asparagus Bundles

### Prep time: 10 minutes | Cook time: 14 minutes | Serves 2

230 g asparagus, trimmed
1 teaspoon extra-virgin olive oil, divided
Salt and pepper, to taste
4 (85 g) skinless sole fillets, ⅛ to ¼ inch thick
4 tablespoons unsalted butter,

softened
1 small shallot, minced
1 tablespoon chopped fresh tarragon
¼ teaspoon lemon zest plus ½ teaspoon juice
Vegetable oil spray

1. Preheat the air fryer to 150°C. 2. Toss asparagus with ½ teaspoon oil, pinch salt, and pinch pepper in a bowl. Cover and microwave until bright green and just tender, about 3 minutes, tossing halfway through microwaving. Uncover and set aside to cool slightly. 3. Make foil sling for air fryer basket by folding 1 long sheet of aluminum foil so it is 4 inches wide. Lay sheet of foil widthwise across basket, pressing foil into and up sides of basket. Fold excess foil as needed so that edges of foil are flush with top of basket. Lightly spray foil and basket with vegetable oil spray. 4. Pat sole dry with paper towels and season with salt and pepper. Arrange fillets skinned side up on cutting board, with thicker ends closest to you. Arrange asparagus evenly across base of each fillet, then tightly roll fillets away from you around asparagus to form tidy bundles. 5. Rub bundles evenly with remaining ½ teaspoon oil and

arrange seam side down on sling in prepared basket. Bake until asparagus is tender and sole flakes apart when gently prodded with a paring knife, 14 to 18 minutes, using a sling to rotate bundles halfway through cooking. 6. Combine butter, shallot, tarragon, and lemon zest and juice in a bowl. Using sling, carefully remove sole bundles from air fryer and transfer to individual plates. Top evenly with butter mixture and serve.

## Lemony Prawns and Courgette

### Prep time: 15 minutes | Cook time: 7 to 8 minutes | Serves 4

570 g extra-large raw prawns, peeled and deveined
2 medium courgettes (about 230 g each), halved lengthwise and cut into ½-inch-thick slices
1½ tablespoons olive oil
½ teaspoon garlic salt

1½ teaspoons dried oregano
⅛ teaspoon crushed red pepper flakes (optional)
Juice of ½ lemon
1 tablespoon chopped fresh mint
1 tablespoon chopped fresh dill

1. Preheat the air fryer to 180°C. 2. In a large bowl, combine the prawns, courgette, oil, garlic salt, oregano, and pepper flakes (if using) and toss to coat. 3. Working in batches, arrange a single layer of the prawns and courgette in the air fryer basket. Air fry for 7 to 8 minutes, shaking the basket halfway, until the courgette is golden and the prawns are cooked through. 4. Transfer to a serving dish and tent with foil while you air fry the remaining prawns and courgette. 5. Top with the lemon juice, mint, and dill and serve.

## Crab-Stuffed Avocado Boats

### Prep time: 5 minutes | Cook time: 7 minutes | Serves 4

2 medium avocados, halved and pitted
230 g cooked crab meat
¼ teaspoon Old Bay seasoning

2 tablespoons peeled and diced yellow onion
2 tablespoons mayonnaise

1. Scoop out avocado flesh in each avocado half, leaving ½ inch around edges to form a shell. Chop scooped-out avocado. 2. In a medium bowl, combine crab meat, Old Bay seasoning, onion, mayonnaise, and chopped avocado. Place ¼ mixture into each avocado shell. 3. Place avocado boats into ungreased air fryer basket. Adjust the temperature to 180°C and air fry for 7 minutes. Avocado will be browned on the top and mixture will be bubbling when done. Serve warm.

# Simple Buttery Cod

**Prep time: 5 minutes | Cook time: 8 minutes | Serves 2**

2 cod fillets, 110 g each
2 tablespoons salted butter, melted

1 teaspoon Old Bay seasoning
½ medium lemon, sliced

1. Place cod fillets into a round baking dish. Brush each fillet with butter and sprinkle with Old Bay seasoning. Lay two lemon slices on each fillet. Cover the dish with foil and place into the air fryer basket. 2. Adjust the temperature to 180°C and bake for 8 minutes. Flip halfway through the cooking time. When cooked, internal temperature should be at least 64°C. Serve warm.

# Blackened Red Snapper

**Prep time: 13 minutes | Cook time: 8 to 10 minutes | Serves 4**

1½ teaspoons black pepper
¼ teaspoon thyme
¼ teaspoon garlic powder
⅛ teaspoon cayenne pepper
1 teaspoon olive oil

4 red snapper fillet portions, skin on, 110 g each
4 thin slices lemon
Cooking spray

1. Mix the spices and oil together to make a paste. Rub into both sides of the fish. 2. Spray the air fryer basket with nonstick cooking spray and lay snapper steaks in basket, skin-side down. 3. Place a lemon slice on each piece of fish. 4. Roast at 200°C for 8 to 10 minutes. The fish will not flake when done, but it should be white through the center.

# Almond-Crusted Fish

**Prep time: 15 minutes | Cook time: 10 minutes | Serves 4**

4 firm white fish fillets, 110g each
25 g breadcrumbs
20 g slivered almonds, crushed
2 tablespoons lemon juice
⅛ teaspoon cayenne

Salt and pepper, to taste
470 g plain flour
1 egg, beaten with 1 tablespoon water
Olive or vegetable oil for misting or cooking spray

1. Split fish fillets lengthwise down the center to create 8 pieces. 2. Mix breadcrumbs and almonds together and set aside. 3. Mix the lemon juice and cayenne together. Brush on all sides of fish. 4. Season fish to taste with salt and pepper. 5. Place the flour on a sheet of wax paper. 6. Roll fillets in flour, dip in egg wash, and roll in the crumb mixture. 7. Mist both sides of fish with oil or cooking spray. 8. Spray the air fryer basket and lay fillets inside. 9. Roast at 200°C for 5 minutes, turn fish over, and cook for an additional 5 minutes or until fish is done and flakes easily.

# Sea Bass with Roasted Root Vegetables

**Prep time: 10 minutes | Cook time: 15 minutes | Serves 4**

1 carrot, diced small
1 parsnip, diced small
1 swede, diced small
60 ml olive oil
1 teaspoon salt, divided

4 sea bass fillets
½ teaspoon onion powder
2 garlic cloves, minced
1 lemon, sliced, plus additional wedges for serving

1. Preheat the air fryer to 190°C. 2. In a small bowl, toss the carrot, parsnip, and swede with olive oil and 1 teaspoon salt. 3. Lightly season the sea bass with the remaining 1 teaspoon of salt and the onion powder, then place it into the air fryer basket in a single layer. 4. Spread the garlic over the top of each fillet, then cover with lemon slices. 5. Pour the prepared vegetables into the basket around and on top of the fish. Roast for 15 minutes. 6. Serve with additional lemon wedges if desired.

# Salmon Spring Rolls

**Prep time: 20 minutes | Cook time: 8 to 10 minutes | Serves 4**

230 g salmon fillet
1 teaspoon toasted sesame oil
1 onion, sliced
8 rice paper wrappers
1 yellow bell pepper, thinly

sliced
1 carrot, shredded
10 g chopped fresh flat-leaf parsley
15 g chopped fresh basil

1. Put the salmon in the air fryer basket and drizzle with the sesame oil. Add the onion. Air fry at 190°C for 8 to 10 minutes, or until the salmon just flakes when tested with a fork and the onion is tender. 2. Meanwhile, fill a small shallow bowl with warm water. One at a time, dip the rice paper wrappers into the water and place on a work surface. 3. Top each wrapper with one-eighth each of the salmon and onion mixture, yellow bell pepper, carrot, parsley, and basil. Roll up the wrapper, folding in the sides, to enclose the ingredients. 4. If you like, bake in the air fryer at 190°C for 7 to 9 minutes, until the rolls are crunchy. Cut the rolls in half to serve.

## Prawn Dejonghe Skewers

**Prep time: 10 minutes | Cook time: 15 minutes | Serves 4**

| | |
|---|---|
| 2 teaspoons sherry, or apple cider vinegar | plus more for garnish |
| 3 tablespoons unsalted butter, melted | 1 teaspoon kosher salt |
| 60 g panko bread crumbs | Pinch of cayenne pepper |
| 3 cloves garlic, minced | 680 g prawns, peeled and deveined |
| 8 g minced flat-leaf parsley, | Vegetable oil, for spraying |
| | Lemon wedges, for serving |

1. Stir the sherry and melted butter together in a shallow bowl or pie plate and whisk until combined. Set aside. Whisk together the panko, garlic, parsley, salt, and cayenne pepper on a large plate or shallow bowl. 2. Thread the prawns onto metal skewers designed for the air fryer or bamboo skewers, 3 to 4 per skewer. Dip 1 prawns skewer in the butter mixture, then dredge in the panko mixture until each prawns is lightly coated. Place the skewer on a plate or rimmed baking sheet and repeat the process with the remaining skewers. 3. Preheat the air fryer to 180ºC. Arrange 4 skewers in the air fryer basket. Spray the skewers with oil and air fry for 8 minutes, until the bread crumbs are golden brown and the prawns are cooked through. Transfer the cooked skewers to a serving plate and keep warm while cooking the remaining 4 skewers in the air fryer. 4. Sprinkle the cooked skewers with additional fresh parsley and serve with lemon wedges if desired.

## Cod Tacos with Mango Salsa

**Prep time: 15 minutes | Cook time: 17 minutes | Serves 4**

| | |
|---|---|
| 1 mango, peeled and diced | 1 egg |
| 1 small jalapeño pepper, diced | 75 g cornflour |
| ½ red bell pepper, diced | 90 g plain flour |
| ½ red onion, minced | ½ teaspoon ground cumin |
| Pinch chopped fresh cilantro | ¼ teaspoon chilli powder |
| Juice of ½ lime | 455 g cod, cut into 4 pieces |
| ¼ teaspoon salt | Olive oil spray |
| ¼ teaspoon ground black pepper | 4 corn tortillas, or flour tortillas, at room temperature |
| 120 ml Mexican beer | |

1. In a small bowl, stir together the mango, jalapeño, red bell pepper, red onion, cilantro, lime juice, salt, and pepper. Set aside. 2. In a medium bowl, whisk the beer and egg. 3. In another medium bowl, stir together the cornflour, flour, cumin, and chilli powder. 4. Insert the crisper plate into the basket and the basket into the unit. Preheat the unit to 190ºC. 5. Dip the fish pieces into the egg mixture and in the flour mixture to coat completely. 6. Once the unit is preheated, place a baking paper liner into the basket. Place the fish on the liner in a single layer. 7. Cook for about 9 minutes, spray the fish with olive oil. Reinsert the basket to resume cooking. 8. When the cooking is complete, the fish should be golden and crispy. Place the pieces in the tortillas, top with the mango salsa, and serve.

## Fish Croquettes with Lemon-Dill Aioli

**Prep time: 15 minutes | Cook time: 10 minutes | Serves 4**

| | |
|---|---|
| Croquettes: | tablespoons, divided |
| 3 large eggs, divided | 1 teaspoon fresh lemon juice |
| 340 g raw cod fillet, flaked apart with two forks | 1 teaspoon kosher or coarse sea salt |
| 60 ml skimmed milk | ½ teaspoon dried thyme |
| 190 g boxed instant mashed potatoes | ¼ teaspoon freshly ground black pepper |
| 2 teaspoons olive oil | Cooking spray |
| 8 g chopped fresh dill | Lemon-Dill Aioli: |
| 1 shallot, minced | 5 tablespoons mayonnaise |
| 1 large garlic clove, minced | Juice of ½ lemon |
| 60 g breadcrumbs plus 2 | 1 tablespoon chopped fresh dill |

1. For the croquettes: In a medium bowl, lightly beat 2 of the eggs. Add the fish, milk, instant mashed potatoes, olive oil, dill, shallot, and garlic, 2 tablespoons of the bread crumbs, lemon juice, salt, thyme, and pepper. Mix to thoroughly combine. Place in the refrigerator for 30 minutes. 2. For the lemon-dill aioli: In a small bowl, combine the mayonnaise, lemon juice, and dill. Set aside. 3. Measure out about 3½ tablespoons of the fish mixture and gently roll in your hands to form a log about 3 inches long. Repeat to make a total of 12 logs. 4. Beat the remaining egg in a small bowl. Place the remaining ¾ cup bread crumbs in a separate bowl. Dip the croquettes in the egg, then coat in the bread crumbs, gently pressing to adhere. Place on a work surface and spray both sides with cooking spray. 5. Preheat the air fryer to 180ºC. 6. Working in batches, arrange a single layer of the croquettes in the air fryer basket. Air fry for about 10 minutes, flipping halfway, until golden. 7. Serve with the aioli for dipping.

# Browned Prawns Patties

**Prep time: 15 minutes | Cook time: 10 to 12 minutes | Serves 4**

230 g raw prawns, peeled, deveined and chopped finely

500 g cooked sushi rice

35 g chopped red bell pepper

35 g chopped celery

35 g chopped spring onion

2 teaspoons Worcestershire sauce

½ teaspoon salt

½ teaspoon garlic powder

½ teaspoon Old Bay seasoning

75 g plain bread crumbs

Cooking spray

1. Preheat the air fryer to 200ºC. 2. Put all the ingredients except the bread crumbs and oil in a large bowl and stir to incorporate. 3. Scoop out the prawn mixture and shape into 8 equal-sized patties with your hands, no more than ½-inch thick. Roll the patties in the bread crumbs on a plate and spray both sides with cooking spray. 4. Place the patties in the air fryer basket. You may need to work in batches to avoid overcrowding. 5. Air fry for 10 to 12 minutes, flipping the patties halfway through, or until the outside is crispy brown. 6. Divide the patties among four plates and serve warm.

# Chapter 6 Beef, Pork, and Lamb

# Chapter 6 Beef, Pork, and Lamb

## Cheddar Bacon Burst with Spinach

**Prep time: 5 minutes | Cook time: 60 minutes |**
**Serves 8**

30 slices bacon

1 tablespoon Chipotle chilli powder

2 teaspoons Italian seasoning

120 g Cheddar cheese

1 kg raw spinach

1. Preheat the air fryer to 190ºC. 2. Weave the bacon into 15 vertical pieces and 12 horizontal pieces. Cut the extra 3 in half to fill in the rest, horizontally. 3. Season the bacon with Chipotle chilli powder and Italian seasoning. 4. Add the cheese to the bacon. 5. Add the spinach and press down to compress. 6. Tightly roll up the woven bacon. 7. Line a baking sheet with kitchen foil and add plenty of salt to it. 8. Put the bacon on top of a cooling rack and put that on top of the baking sheet. 9. Bake for 60 minutes. 10. Let cool for 15 minutes before slicing and serving.

## Pork Loin with Aloha Salsa

**Prep time: 20 minutes | Cook time: 7 to 9 minutes |**
**Serves 4**

Aloha Salsa:

235 g fresh pineapple, chopped in small pieces

60 g red onion, finely chopped

60 g green or red pepper, chopped

½ teaspoon ground cinnamon

1 teaspoon reduced-salt soy sauce

⅛ teaspoon crushed red pepper

⅛ teaspoon ground black pepper

2 eggs

2 tablespoons milk

30 g flour

30 g panko bread crumbs

4 teaspoons sesame seeds

450 g boneless, thin pork loin or tenderloin (⅜- to ½-inch thick)

Pepper and salt

30 g cornflour

Oil for misting or cooking spray

1. In a medium bowl, stir together all ingredients for salsa. Cover and refrigerate while cooking pork. 2. Preheat the air fryer to 200ºC. 3. Beat together eggs and milk in shallow dish. 4. In another shallow dish, mix together the flour, panko, and sesame seeds. 5.

Sprinkle pork with pepper and salt to taste. 6. Dip pork in cornflour, egg mixture, and then panko coating. Spray both sides with oil or cooking spray. 7. Cook pork for 3 minutes. Turn pork over, spraying both sides, and continue cooking for 4 to 6 minutes or until well done. 8. Serve fried cutlets with salsa on the side.

## Italian Pork Loin

**Prep time: 30 minutes | Cook time: 16 minutes |**
**Serves 3**

1 teaspoon sea salt

½ teaspoon black pepper, freshly cracked

60 ml red wine

2 tablespoons mustard

2 garlic cloves, minced

450 g pork loin joint

1 tablespoon Italian herb seasoning blend

1. In a ceramic bowl, mix the salt, black pepper, red wine, mustard, and garlic. Add the pork loin and let it marinate at least 30 minutes. 2. Spritz the sides and bottom of the air fryer basket with nonstick cooking spray. 3. Place the pork loin in the basket; sprinkle with the Italian herb seasoning blend. Cook the pork loin at 190ºC for 10 minutes. Flip halfway through, spraying with cooking oil and cook for 5 to 6 minutes more. Serve immediately.

## Kale and Beef Omelet

**Prep time: 15 minutes | Cook time: 16 minutes |**
**Serves 4**

230 g leftover beef, coarsely chopped

2 garlic cloves, pressed

235 g kale, torn into pieces and wilted

1 tomato, chopped

¼ teaspoon sugar

4 eggs, beaten

4 tablespoons double cream

½ teaspoon turmeric powder

Salt and ground black pepper, to taste

⅛ teaspoon ground allspice

Cooking spray

1. Preheat the air fryer to 180ºC. Spritz four ramekins with cooking spray. 2. Put equal amounts of each of the ingredients into each ramekin and mix well. 3. Air fry for 16 minutes. Serve immediately.

## Sesame Beef Lettuce Tacos

**Prep time: 30 minutes | Cook time: 8 to 10 minutes | Serves 4**

| | |
|---|---|
| 60 ml soy sauce or tamari | 450 g bavette or skirt steak |
| 60 ml avocado oil | 8 butterhead lettuce leaves |
| 2 tablespoons cooking sherry | 2 spring onions, sliced |
| 1 tablespoon granulated sweetener | 1 tablespoon toasted sesame seeds |
| 1 tablespoon ground cumin | Hot sauce, for serving |
| 1 teaspoon minced garlic | Lime wedges, for serving |
| Sea salt and freshly ground black pepper, to taste | Flaky sea salt (optional) |

1. In a small bowl, whisk together the soy sauce, avocado oil, cooking sherry, sweetener, cumin, garlic, and salt and pepper to taste. 2. Place the steak in a shallow dish. Pour the marinade over the beef. Cover the dish with plastic wrap and let it marinate in the refrigerator for at least 2 hours or overnight. 3. Remove the flank steak from the dish and discard the marinade. 4. Set the air fryer to 200ºC. Place the steak in the air fryer basket and air fry for 4 to 6 minutes. Flip the steak and cook for 4 minutes more, until an instant-read thermometer reads 49ºC at the thickest part (or cook it to your desired doneness). Allow the steak to rest for 10 minutes, then slice it thinly against the grain. 5. Stack 2 lettuce leaves on top of each other and add some sliced meat. Top with spring onions and sesame seeds. Drizzle with hot sauce and lime juice, and finish with a little flaky salt (if using). Repeat with the remaining lettuce leaves and fillings.

## Bacon, Cheese and Pear Stuffed Pork

**Prep time: 10 minutes | Cook time: 24 minutes | Serves 3**

| | |
|---|---|
| 4 slices bacon, chopped | ⅛ teaspoon black pepper |
| 1 tablespoon butter | 1 pear, finely diced |
| 120 g finely diced onion | 80 g crumbled blue cheese |
| 80 g chicken stock | 3 boneless pork chops (2-inch thick) |
| 355 g seasoned stuffing mix | |
| 1 egg, beaten | Olive oil |
| ½ teaspoon dried thyme | Salt and freshly ground black pepper, to taste |
| ½ teaspoon salt | |

1. Preheat the air fryer to 200ºC. 2. Place the bacon into the air fryer basket and air fry for 6 minutes, stirring halfway through the cooking time. Remove the bacon and set it aside on a paper towel. Pour out the grease from the bottom of the air fryer. 3. Make the stuffing: Melt the butter in a medium saucepan over medium heat on the stovetop. Add the onion and sauté for a few minutes, until it starts to soften. Add the chicken stock and simmer for 1 minute. Remove the pan from the heat and add the stuffing mix. Stir until the stock has been absorbed. Add the egg, dried thyme, salt and freshly ground black pepper, and stir until combined. Fold in the diced pear and crumbled blue cheese. 4. Place the pork chops on a cutting board. Using the palm of your hand to hold the chop flat and steady, slice into the side of the pork chop to make a pocket in the center of the chop. Leave about an inch of chop uncut and make sure you don't cut all the way through the pork chop. Brush both sides of the pork chops with olive oil and season with salt and freshly ground black pepper. Stuff each pork chop with a third of the stuffing, packing the stuffing tightly inside the pocket. 5. Preheat the air fryer to 180ºC. 6. Spray or brush the sides of the air fryer basket with oil. Place the pork chops in the air fryer basket with the open stuffed edge of the pork chop facing the outside edges of the basket. 7. Air fry the pork chops for 18 minutes, turning the pork chops over halfway through the cooking time. When the chops are done, let them rest for 5 minutes and then transfer to a serving platter.

## Sausage-Stuffed Peppers

**Prep time: 15 minutes | Cook time: 28 to 30 minutes | Serves 6**

| | |
|---|---|
| Avocado oil spray | black pepper, to taste |
| 230 g Italian-seasoned sausage, casings removed | 235 ml keto-friendly marinara sauce |
| 120 g chopped mushrooms | 3 peppers, halved and seeded |
| 60 g diced onion | 85 g low-moisture Mozzarella or other melting cheese, shredded |
| 1 teaspoon Italian seasoning | |
| Sea salt and freshly ground | |

1. Spray a large skillet with oil and place it over medium-high heat. Add the sausage and cook for 5 minutes, breaking up the meat with a wooden spoon. Add the mushrooms, onion, and Italian seasoning, and season with salt and pepper. Cook for 5 minutes more. Stir in the marinara sauce and cook until heated through. 2. Scoop the sausage filling into the pepper halves. 3. Set the air fryer to 180ºC. Arrange the peppers in a single layer in the air fryer basket, working in batches if necessary. Air fry for 15 minutes. 4. Top the stuffed peppers with the cheese and air fry for 3 to 5 minutes more, until the cheese is melted and the peppers are tender.

# Cheese Wine Pork Loin

### Prep time: 30 minutes | Cook time: 15 minutes | Serves 2

| | |
|---|---|
| 235 ml water | ½ teaspoon porcini powder |
| 235 ml red wine | Sea salt and ground black |
| 1 tablespoon sea salt | pepper, to taste |
| 2 pork loin steaks | 1 egg |
| 60 g ground almonds | 60 ml yoghurt |
| 30 g flaxseed meal | 1 teaspoon wholegrain or |
| ½ teaspoon baking powder | English mustard |
| 1 teaspoon onion granules | 80 g Parmesan cheese, grated |

1. In a large ceramic dish, combine the water, wine and salt. Add the pork and put for 1 hour in the refrigerator. 2. In a shallow bowl, mix the ground almonds, flaxseed meal, baking powder, onion granules, porcini powder, salt, and ground pepper. In another bowl, whisk the eggs with yoghurt and mustard. 3. In a third bowl, place the grated Parmesan cheese. 4. Dip the pork in the seasoned flour mixture and toss evenly; then, in the egg mixture. Finally, roll them over the grated Parmesan cheese. 5. Spritz the bottom of the air fryer basket with cooking oil. Add the breaded pork and cook at 200ºC and for 10 minutes. 6. Flip and cook for 5 minutes more on the other side. Serve warm.

# Pork and Beef Egg Rolls

### Prep time: 30 minutes | Cook time: 7 to 8 minutes per batch | Makes 8 egg rolls

| | |
|---|---|
| 110 g very lean beef mince | ¼ teaspoon salt |
| 110 g lean pork mince | ¼ teaspoon garlic powder |
| 1 tablespoon soy sauce | ¼ teaspoon black pepper |
| 1 teaspoon olive oil | 1 egg |
| 120 g grated carrots | 1 tablespoon water |
| 2 green onions, chopped | 8 egg roll wrappers |
| 475 g grated Chinese cabbage | Oil for misting or cooking spray |
| 60 g chopped water chestnuts | |

1. In a large skillet, brown beef and pork with soy sauce. Remove cooked meat from skillet, drain, and set aside. 2. Pour off any excess grease from skillet. Add olive oil, carrots, and onions. Sauté until barely tender, about 1 minute. 3. Stir in cabbage, cover, and cook for 1 minute or just until cabbage slightly wilts. Remove from heat. 4. In a large bowl, combine the cooked meats and vegetables, water chestnuts, salt, garlic powder, and pepper. Stir well. If needed, add more salt to taste. 5. Beat together egg and water in a small bowl. 6. Fill egg roll wrappers, using about 60 ml of filling for each wrap. Roll up and brush all over with egg wash to seal. Spray very lightly with olive oil or cooking spray. 7. Place 4 egg rolls in air fryer basket and air fry at 200ºC for 4 minutes. Turn over and cook 3 to 4 more minutes, until golden brown and crispy. 8. Repeat to cook remaining egg rolls.

# Filipino Crispy Pork Belly

### Prep time: 20 minutes | Cook time: 30 minutes | Serves 4

| | |
|---|---|
| 450 g pork belly | 1 teaspoon coarse or flaky salt |
| 700 ml water | 1 teaspoon black pepper |
| 6 garlic cloves | 2 bay leaves |
| 2 tablespoons soy sauce | |

1. Cut the pork belly into three thick chunks so it will cook more evenly. 2. Place the pork, water, garlic, soy sauce, salt, pepper, and bay leaves in the inner pot of an Instant Pot or other electric pressure cooker. Seal and cook at high pressure for 15 minutes. Let the pressure release naturally for 10 minutes, then manually release the remaining pressure. (If you do not have a pressure cooker, place all the ingredients in a large saucepan. Cover and cook over low heat until a knife can be easily inserted into the skin side of pork belly, about 1 hour.) Using tongs, very carefully transfer the meat to a wire rack over a rimmed baking sheet to drain and dry for 10 minutes. 3. Cut each chunk of pork belly into two long slices. Arrange the slices in the air fryer basket. Set the air fryer to 200ºC for 15 minutes, or until the fat has crisped. 4. Serve immediately.

# Herb-Roasted Beef Tips with Onions

### Prep time: 5 minutes | Cook time: 10 minutes | Serves 4

| | |
|---|---|
| 450 g rib eye steak, cubed | 1 teaspoon salt |
| 2 garlic cloves, minced | ½ teaspoon black pepper |
| 2 tablespoons olive oil | 1 brown onion, thinly sliced |
| 1 tablespoon fresh oregano | |

1. Preheat the air fryer to 190ºC. 2. In a medium bowl, combine the steak, garlic, olive oil, oregano, salt, pepper, and onion. Mix until all of the beef and onion are well coated. 3. Put the seasoned steak mixture into the air fryer basket. Roast for 5 minutes. Stir and roast for 5 minutes more. 4. Let rest for 5 minutes before serving with some favourite sides.

# Rack of Lamb with Pistachio Crust

**Prep time: 10 minutes | Cook time: 19 minutes |**

**Serves 2**

120 g finely chopped pistachios

3 tablespoons panko bread crumbs

1 teaspoon chopped fresh rosemary

2 teaspoons chopped fresh oregano

Salt and freshly ground black pepper, to taste

1 tablespoon olive oil

1 rack of lamb, bones trimmed of fat and frenched

1 tablespoon Dijon mustard

1. Preheat the air fryer to 190ºC. 2. Combine the pistachios, bread crumbs, rosemary, oregano, salt and pepper in a small bowl. (This is a good job for your food processor if you have one.) Drizzle in the olive oil and stir to combine. 3. Season the rack of lamb with salt and pepper on all sides and transfer it to the air fryer basket with the fat side facing up. Air fry the lamb for 12 minutes. Remove the lamb from the air fryer and brush the fat side of the lamb rack with the Dijon mustard. Coat the rack with the pistachio mixture, pressing the bread crumbs onto the lamb with your hands and rolling the bottom of the rack in any of the crumbs that fall off. 4. Return the rack of lamb to the air fryer and air fry for another 3 to 7 minutes or until an instant read thermometer reads 60ºC for medium. Add or subtract a couple of minutes for lamb that is more or less well cooked. (Your time will vary depending on how big the rack of lamb is.) 5. Let the lamb rest for at least 5 minutes. Then, slice into chops and serve.

# Beef Bavette Steak with Sage

**Prep time: 13 minutes | Cook time: 7 minutes |**

**Serves 2**

80 ml sour cream

120 g spring onion, chopped

1 tablespoon mayonnaise

3 cloves garlic, smashed

450 g beef bavette or skirt steak, trimmed and cubed

2 tablespoons fresh sage, minced

½ teaspoon salt

⅓ teaspoon black pepper, or to taste

1. Season your meat with salt and pepper; arrange beef cubes on the bottom of a baking dish that fits in your air fryer. 2. Stir in spring onions and garlic; air fry for about 7 minutes at 200ºC. 3. Once your beef starts to tender, add the cream, mayonnaise, and sage; air fry an additional 8 minutes. Bon appétit!

# Sausage and Pork Meatballs

**Prep time: 15 minutes | Cook time: 8 to 12 minutes |**

**Serves 8**

1 large egg

1 teaspoon gelatin

450 g pork mince

230 g Italian-seasoned sausage, casings removed, crumbled

80 g Parmesan cheese

60 g finely diced onion

1 tablespoon tomato paste

1 teaspoon minced garlic

1 teaspoon dried oregano

¼ teaspoon red pepper flakes

Sea salt and freshly ground black pepper, to taste

Keto-friendly marinara sauce, for serving

1. Beat the egg in a small bowl and sprinkle with the gelatin. Allow to sit for 5 minutes. 2. In a large bowl, combine the pork mince, sausage, Parmesan, onion, tomato paste, garlic, oregano, and red pepper flakes. Season with salt and black pepper. 3. Stir the gelatin mixture, then add it to the other ingredients and, using clean hands, mix to ensure that everything is well combined. Form into 1½-inch round meatballs. 4. Set the air fryer to 200ºC. Place the meatballs in the air fryer basket in a single layer, cooking in batches as needed. Air fry for 5 minutes. Flip and cook for 3 to 7 minutes more, or until an instant-read thermometer reads 72ºC.

# Sumptuous Pizza Tortilla Rolls

**Prep time: 10 minutes | Cook time: 6 minutes |**

**Serves 4**

1 teaspoon butter

½ medium onion, slivered

½ red or green pepper, julienned

110 g fresh white mushrooms, chopped

120 ml pizza sauce

8 flour tortillas

8 thin slices wafer-thinham

24 pepperoni slices

235 g shredded Mozzarella cheese

Cooking spray

1. Preheat the air fryer to 200ºC. 2. Put butter, onions, pepper, and mushrooms in a baking tray. Bake in the preheated air fryer for 3 minutes. Stir and cook 3 to 4 minutes longer until just crisp and tender. Remove pan and set aside. 3. To assemble rolls, spread about 2 teaspoons of pizza sauce on one half of each tortilla. Top with a slice of ham and 3 slices of pepperoni. Divide sautéed vegetables among tortillas and top with cheese. 4. Roll up tortillas, secure with toothpicks if needed, and spray with oil. 5. Put 4 rolls in air fryer basket and air fry for 4 minutes. Turn and air fry 4 minutes, until heated through and lightly browned. 6. Repeat step 4 to air fry remaining pizza rolls. 7. Serve immediately.

# Italian Lamb Chops with Avocado Mayo

**Prep time: 5 minutes | Cook time: 12 minutes | Serves 2**

2 lamp chops
2 teaspoons Italian herbs
2 avocados
120 ml mayonnaise
1 tablespoon lemon juice

1. Season the lamb chops with the Italian herbs, then set aside for 5 minutes. 2. Preheat the air fryer to 200°C and place the rack inside. 3. Put the chops on the rack and air fry for 12 minutes. 4. In the meantime, halve the avocados and open to remove the pits. Spoon the flesh into a blender. 5. Add the mayonnaise and lemon juice and pulse until a smooth consistency is achieved. 6. Take care when removing the chops from the air fryer, then plate up and serve with the avocado mayo.

# Mexican Pork Chops

**Prep time: 5 minutes | Cook time: 15 minutes | Serves 2**

¼ teaspoon dried oregano
1½ teaspoons taco seasoning or fajita seasoning mix
2 (110 g) boneless pork chops
2 tablespoons unsalted butter, divided

1. Preheat the air fryer to 200°C. 2. Combine the dried oregano and taco seasoning in a small bowl and rub the mixture into the pork chops. Brush the chops with 1 tablespoon butter. 3. In the air fryer, air fry the chops for 15 minutes, turning them over halfway through to air fry on the other side. 4. When the chops are a brown color, check the internal temperature has reached 64°C and remove from the air fryer. Serve with a garnish of remaining butter.

# Beef and Pork Sausage Meatloaf

**Prep time: 20 minutes | Cook time: 25 minutes | Serves 4**

340 g beef mince
110 g pork sausage meat
235 g shallots, finely chopped
2 eggs, well beaten
3 tablespoons milk
1 tablespoon oyster sauce
1 teaspoon porcini mushrooms
½ teaspoon cumin powder
1 teaspoon garlic paste
1 tablespoon fresh parsley
Salt and crushed red pepper flakes, to taste

235 g crushed cream crackers      Cooking spray

1. Preheat the air fryer to 180°C. Spritz a baking dish with cooking spray. 2. Mix all the ingredients in a large bowl, combining everything well. 3. Transfer to the baking dish and bake in the air fryer for 25 minutes. 4. Serve hot.

# Beef and Goat Cheese Stuffed Peppers

**Prep time: 10 minutes | Cook time: 30 minutes | Serves 4**

450 g lean beef mince
120 g cooked brown rice
2 plum tomatoes, diced
3 garlic cloves, minced
½ brown onion, diced
2 tablespoons fresh oregano, chopped
1 teaspoon salt
½ teaspoon black pepper
¼ teaspoon ground allspice
2 peppers, halved and seeded
110 g goat cheese
60 g fresh parsley, chopped

1. Preheat the air fryer to 180°C. 2. In a large bowl, combine the beef, rice, tomatoes, garlic, onion, oregano, salt, pepper, and allspice. Mix well. 3. Divide the beef mixture equally into the halved peppers and top each with about a quarter of the goat cheese. 4. Place the peppers into the air fryer basket in a single layer, making sure that they don't touch each other. Bake for 30 minutes. 5. Remove the peppers from the air fryer and top with fresh parsley before serving.

# Greek Lamb Rack

**Prep time: 5 minutes | Cook time: 10 minutes | Serves 4**

60 g freshly squeezed lemon juice
1 teaspoon oregano
2 teaspoons minced fresh rosemary
1 teaspoon minced fresh thyme
2 tablespoons minced garlic
Salt and freshly ground black pepper, to taste
2 to 4 tablespoons olive oil
1 lamb rib rack (7 to 8 ribs)

1. Preheat the air fryer to 180°C. 2. In a small mixing bowl, combine the lemon juice, oregano, rosemary, thyme, garlic, salt, pepper, and olive oil and mix well. 3. Rub the mixture over the lamb, covering all the meat. Put the rack of lamb in the air fryer. Roast for 10 minutes. Flip the rack halfway through. 4. After 10 minutes, measure the internal temperature of the rack of lamb reaches at least 64°C. 5. Serve immediately.

# Air Fryer Chicken-Fried Steak

**Prep time: 5 minutes | Cook time: 20 minutes |**
**Serves 4**

| | |
|---|---|
| 450 g beef braising steak | 2 medium egg whites |
| 700 ml low-fat milk, divided | 120 g gluten-free breadcrumbs |
| 1 teaspoon dried thyme | 60 g coconut flour |
| 1 teaspoon dried rosemary | 1 tablespoon Cajun seasoning |

1. In a bowl, marinate the steak in 475 ml of milk for 30 to 45 minutes. 2. Remove the steak from milk, shake off the excess liquid, and season with the thyme and rosemary. Discard the milk. 3. In a shallow bowl, beat the egg whites with the remaining 235 ml of milk. 4. In a separate shallow bowl, combine the breadcrumbs, coconut flour, and seasoning. 5. Dip the steak in the egg white mixture then dredge in the breadcrumb mixture, coating well. 6. Place the steak in the basket of an air fryer. 7. Set the air fryer to 200ºC, close, and cook for 10 minutes. 8. Open the air fryer, turn the steaks, close, and cook for 10 minutes. Let rest for 5 minutes.

# Pork Tenderloin with Avocado Lime Sauce

**Prep time: 30 minutes | Cook time: 15 minutes |**
**Serves 4**

| | |
|---|---|
| Marinade: | 120 ml full-fat sour cream (or |
| 120 ml lime juice | coconut cream for dairy-free) |
| Grated zest of 1 lime | Grated zest of 1 lime |
| 2 teaspoons stevia glycerite, or | Juice of 1 lime |
| ¼ teaspoon liquid stevia | 2 cloves garlic, roughly |
| 3 cloves garlic, minced | chopped |
| 1½ teaspoons fine sea salt | ½ teaspoon fine sea salt |
| 1 teaspoon chili powder, or | ¼ teaspoon ground black |
| more for more heat | pepper |
| 1 teaspoon smoked paprika | Chopped fresh coriander leaves, |
| 450 g pork tenderloin | for garnish |
| Avocado Lime Sauce: | Lime slices, for serving |
| 1 medium-sized ripe avocado, | Pico de gallo or salsa, for |
| roughly chopped | serving |

1. In a medium-sized casserole dish, stir together all the marinade ingredients until well combined. Add the tenderloin and coat it well in the marinade. Cover and place in the fridge to marinate for 2 hours or overnight. 2. Spray the air fryer basket with avocado oil. Preheat the air fryer to 200ºC. 3. Remove the pork from the marinade and place it in the air fryer basket. Air fry for 13 to 15 minutes, until the internal temperature of the pork is 64ºC, flipping after 7 minutes. Remove the pork from the air fryer and place it on a cutting board. Allow it to rest for 8 to 10 minutes, then cut it into ½-inch-thick slices. 4. While the pork cooks, make the avocado lime sauce: Place all the sauce ingredients in a food processor and purée until smooth. Taste and adjust the seasoning to your liking. 5. Place the pork slices on a serving platter and spoon the avocado lime sauce on top. Garnish with coriander leaves and serve with lime slices and pico de gallo. 6. Store leftovers in an airtight container in the fridge for up to 4 days. Reheat in a preheated 200ºC air fryer for 5 minutes, or until heated through.

# Panko Pork Chops

**Prep time: 10 minutes | Cook time: 12 minutes |**
**Serves 4**

| | |
|---|---|
| 4 boneless pork chops, excess | 1½ teaspoons paprika |
| fat trimmed | ½ teaspoon granulated garlic |
| ¼ teaspoon salt | ½ teaspoon onion granules |
| 2 eggs | 1 teaspoon chili powder |
| 130 g panko bread crumbs | ¼ teaspoon freshly ground |
| 3 tablespoons grated Parmesan | black pepper |
| cheese | Olive oil spray |

1. Sprinkle the pork chops with salt on both sides and let them sit while you prepare the seasonings and egg wash. 2. In a shallow medium bowl, beat the eggs. 3. In another shallow medium bowl, stir together the panko, Parmesan cheese, paprika, granulated garlic, onion granules, chili powder, and pepper. 4. Dip the pork chops in the egg and in the panko mixture to coat. Firmly press the crumbs onto the chops. 5. Insert the crisper plate into the basket and the basket into the unit. Preheat the unit by selecting AIR ROAST, setting the temperature to 200ºC, and setting the time to 3 minutes. Select START/STOP to begin. 6. Once the unit is preheated, spray the crisper plate with olive oil. Place the pork chops into the basket and spray them with olive oil. 7. Select AIR ROAST, set the temperature to 200ºC, and set the time to 12 minutes. Select START/STOP to begin. 8. After 6 minutes, flip the pork chops and spray them with more olive oil. Resume cooking. 9. When the cooking is complete, the chops should be golden and crispy and a food thermometer should register 64ºC. Serve immediately.

# Onion Pork Kebabs

**Prep time: 22 minutes | Cook time: 18 minutes | Serves 3**

2 tablespoons tomato purée

½ fresh green chilli, minced

⅓ teaspoon paprika

450 g pork mince

120 g spring onions, finely chopped

3 cloves garlic, peeled and finely minced

1 teaspoon ground black pepper, or more to taste

1 teaspoon salt, or more to taste

1. Thoroughly combine all ingredients in a mixing dish. Then form your mixture into sausage shapes. 2. Cook for 18 minutes at 180°C. Mound salad on a serving platter, top with air-fried kebabs and serve warm. Bon appétit!

# Steak Gyro Platter

**Prep time: 30 minutes | Cook time: 8 to 10 minutes | Serves 4**

450 g bavette or skirt steak

1 teaspoon garlic powder

1 teaspoon ground cumin

½ teaspoon sea salt

½ teaspoon freshly ground black pepper

140 g shredded romaine lettuce

120 g crumbled feta cheese

120 g peeled and diced cucumber

80 g sliced red onion

60 g seeded and diced tomato

2 tablespoons pitted and sliced black olives

Tzatziki sauce, for serving

1. Pat the steak dry with paper towels. In a small bowl, combine the garlic powder, cumin, salt, and pepper. Sprinkle this mixture all over the steak, and allow the steak to rest at room temperature for 45 minutes. 2. Preheat the air fryer to 200°C. Place the steak in the air fryer basket and air fry for 4 minutes. Flip the steak and cook 4 to 6 minutes more, until an instant-read thermometer reads 49°C at the thickest point for medium-rare (or as desired). Remove the steak from the air fryer and let it rest for 5 minutes. 3. Divide the romaine among plates. Top with the feta, cucumber, red onion, tomato, and olives.

# Chapter 7 Snacks and Appetizers

# Chapter 7 Snacks and Appetizers

## Sea Salt Potato Crisps

**Prep time: 30 minutes | Cook time: 27 minutes | Serves 4**

Oil, for spraying
4 medium-sized yellow potatoes such as Maris Piper potatoes

1 tablespoon oil
⅛ to ¼ teaspoon fine sea salt

1. Line the air fryer basket with baking paper and spray lightly with oil. 2. Using a mandoline or a very sharp knife, cut the potatoes into very thin slices. 3. Place the slices in a bowl of cold water and let soak for about 20 minutes. 4. Drain the potatoes, transfer them to a plate lined with kitchen roll, and pat dry. 5. Drizzle the oil over the potatoes, sprinkle with the salt, and toss to combine. Transfer to the prepared basket. 6. Air fry at 90°C for 20 minutes. Toss the crisps, increase the heat to 200°C, and cook for another 5 to 7 minutes, until crispy.

## Cheese Drops

**Prep time: 15 minutes | Cook time: 10 minutes per batch | Serves 8**

90 g plain flour
½ teaspoon rock salt
¼ teaspoon cayenne pepper
¼ teaspoon smoked paprika
¼ teaspoon black pepper
a dash of garlic powder

(optional)
57 g butter, softened
100 g grated extra mature cheddar cheese, at room temperature
Olive oil spray

1. 1.In a small bowl, combine the flour, salt, cayenne, paprika, pepper, and garlic powder, if using. 2. Using a food processor, cream the butter and cheese until smooth. Gently add the seasoned flour and process until the dough is well combined, smooth, and no longer sticky. (Or make the dough in a stand mixer fitted with the paddle attachment: Cream the butter and cheese at medium speed until smooth, then add the seasoned flour and beat at low speed until smooth.) 3. Divide the dough into 32 pieces of equal size. On a lightly floured surface, roll each piece into a small ball. 4. Spray the air fryer basket with oil spray. Arrange 16 cheese drops in the basket. Set the air fryer to 160°C for 10 minutes, or until drops are just starting to brown. Transfer to a a wire rack. Repeat with remaining dough, checking for degree of doneness at 8 minutes. 5. Cool the cheese drops completely on the a wire rack. Store in an airtight container until ready to serve, or up to 1 or 2 days.

## Crispy Chilli Chickpeas

**Prep time: 5 minutes | Cook time: 15 minutes | Serves 4**

1 (425 g) can cooked chickpeas, drained and rinsed
1 tablespoon olive oil
¼ teaspoon salt

⅛ teaspoon chili powder
⅛ teaspoon garlic powder
⅛ teaspoon paprika

1. Preheat the air fryer to 190°C. 2. In a medium-sized bowl, toss all of the ingredients together until the chickpeas are well coated. 3. Pour the chickpeas into the air fryer and spread them out in a single layer. 4. Roast for 15 minutes, stirring once halfway through the cook time.

## Black Bean Corn Dip

**Prep time: 10 minutes | Cook time: 10 minutes | Serves 4**

½ (425 g) can black beans, drained and rinsed
½ (425 g) can sweetcorn, drained and rinsed
60 g chunky salsa
57 g low-fat soft white cheese

40 g shredded low-fat Cheddar cheese
½ teaspoon cumin powder
½ teaspoon paprika
Salt and freshly ground black pepper, to taste

Preheat the air fryer to 160°C. 2. In a medium-sized bowl, mix together the black beans, sweetcorn, salsa, soft white cheese, Cheddar cheese, cumin, and paprika. Season with salt and pepper and stir until well combined. 3. Spoon the mixture into a baking dish. 4. Place baking dish in the air fryer basket and bake until heated through, about 10 minutes. 5. Serve hot.

## Bruschetta with Basil Pesto

**Prep time: 10 minutes | Cook time: 5 to 11 minutes | Serves 4**

| | |
|---|---|
| 8 slices French bread, ½ inch thick | cheese cheese |
| 2 tablespoons softened butter | 120 g basil pesto |
| 120 g shredded mozzarella | 240 g chopped cherry tomatoes |
| | 2 spring onions, thinly sliced |

1. Preheat the air fryer to 180ºC. 2. Spread the bread with the butter and place butter-side up in the air fryer basket. Bake for 3 to 5 minutes, or until the bread is light golden. 3. Remove the bread from the basket and top each piece with some of the cheese. Return to the basket in 2 batches and bake for 1 to 3 minutes, or until the cheese melts. 4. Meanwhile, combine the pesto, tomatoes, and spring onions in a small bowl. 5. When the cheese has melted, remove the bread from the air fryer and place on a serving plate. Top each slice with some of the pesto mixture and serve.

## Greek Potato Skins with Olives and Feta

**Prep time: 5 minutes | Cook time: 45 minutes | Serves 4**

| | |
|---|---|
| 2 russet potatoes or Maris Piper potatoes | 2 tablespoons fresh coriander, chopped, plus more for serving |
| 3 tablespoons olive oil, divided, plus more for drizzling (optional) | 60 g Kalamata olives, diced |
| | 60 g crumbled feta cheese |
| 1 teaspoon rock salt, divided | Chopped fresh parsley, for garnish (optional) |
| ¼ teaspoon black pepper | |

1. Preheat the air fryer to 190ºC. 2. Using a fork, poke 2 to 3 holes in the potatoes, then coat each with about ½ tablespoon olive oil and ½ teaspoon salt. 3. Place the potatoes into the air fryer basket and bake for 30 minutes. 4. Remove the potatoes from the air fryer, and slice in half. Using a spoon, scoop out the flesh of the potatoes, leaving a ½-inch layer of potato inside the skins, and set the skins aside. 5. In a medium-sized bowl, combine the scooped potato middles with the remaining 2 tablespoons of olive oil, ½ teaspoon of salt, black pepper, and coriander. Mix until well combined. 6. Divide the potato filling into the now-empty potato skins, spreading it evenly over them. Top each potato with a tablespoon each of the olives and feta cheese. 7. Place the loaded potato skins back into the air fryer and bake for 15 minutes. 8. Serve with additional chopped coriander or parsley and a drizzle of olive oil, if desired.

## Grilled Ham and Cheese on Raisin Bread

**Prep time: 5 minutes | Cook time: 10 minutes | Serves 1**

| | |
|---|---|
| 2 slices raisin bread or fruit loaf | roast ham (about 85 g) |
| 2 tablespoons butter, softened | 4 slices Muenster cheese (about 85 g) |
| 2 teaspoons honey mustard | |
| 3 slices thinly sliced honey | 2 cocktail sticks |

1. Preheat the air fryer to 190ºC. 2. Spread the softened butter on one side of both slices of bread and place the bread, buttered side down on the counter. Spread the honey mustard on the other side of each slice of bread. Layer 2 slices of cheese, the ham and the remaining 2 slices of cheese on one slice of bread and top with the other slice of bread. Remember to leave the buttered side of the bread on the outside. 3. Transfer the sandwich to the air fryer basket and secure the sandwich with cocktail sticks. 4. Air fry for 5 minutes. Flip the sandwich over, remove the cocktail sticks and air fry for another 5 minutes. Cut the sandwich in half and enjoy!

## Lemon Prawns with Garlic Olive Oil

**Prep time: 5 minutes | Cook time: 6 minutes | Serves 4**

| | |
|---|---|
| 340 g medium prawns, cleaned and deveined | ½ teaspoon salt |
| | ¼ teaspoon red pepper flakes |
| 60 ml plus 2 tablespoons olive oil, divided | Lemon wedges, for serving (optional) |
| Juice of ½ lemon | Marinara sauce, for dipping (optional) |
| 3 garlic cloves, minced and divided | |

1. Preheat the air fryer to 190ºC. 2. In a large bowl, combine the prawns with 2 tablespoons of the olive oil, as well as the lemon juice, ⅓ of the minced garlic, salt, and red pepper flakes. Toss to coat the prawns well. 3. In a small ramekin, combine the remaining 60 ml of olive oil and the remaining minced garlic. 4. Tear off a 12-by-12-inch sheet of aluminium foil. Pour the prawns into the centre of the foil, then fold the sides up and crimp the edges so that it forms an aluminium foil bowl that is open on top. Place this packet into the air fryer basket. 5. Roast the prawns for 4 minutes, then open the air fryer and place the ramekin with oil and garlic in the basket beside the prawns packet. Cook for 2 more minutes. 6. Transfer the prawns on a serving plate or platter with the ramekin of garlic olive oil on the side for dipping. You may also serve with lemon wedges and marinara sauce, if desired.

# Sweet Bacon Potato Crunchies

**Prep time: 5 minutes | Cook time: 7 minutes | Serves 4**

24 frozen potato crisps

6 slices cooked bacon

2 tablespoons maple syrup

110 g shredded Cheddar cheese

1. Preheat the air fryer to 200ºC. 2. Put the potato crisps in the air fryer basket. Air fry for 10 minutes, shaking the basket halfway through the cooking time. 3. Meanwhile, cut the bacon into 1-inch pieces. 4. Remove the potato crisps from the air fryer basket and put into a baking pan. Top with the bacon and drizzle with the maple syrup. Air fry for 5 minutes, or until the crunchies and bacon are crisp. 5. Top with the cheese and air fry for 2 minutes, or until the cheese is melted. 6. Serve hot.

# Prawns Egg Rolls

**Prep time: 15 minutes | Cook time: 10 minutes per batch | Serves 4**

1 tablespoon mixed vegetables oil

½ head green or savoy cabbage, finely shredded

90 g grated carrots

240 ml canned bean sprouts, drained

1 tablespoon soy sauce

½ teaspoon sugar

1 teaspoon sesame oil

60 ml hoisin sauce

Freshly ground black pepper, to taste

454 g cooked prawns, diced

30 g spring onions

8 egg roll wrappers (or use spring roll pastry)

mixed vegetables oil

Duck sauce

1. Preheat a large sauté pan over medium-high heat. Add the oil and cook the cabbage, carrots and bean sprouts until they start to wilt, about 3 minutes. Add the soy sauce, sugar, sesame oil, hoisin sauce and black pepper. Sauté for a few more minutes. Stir in the prawns and spring onions and cook until the mixed vegetables are just tender. Transfer the mixture to a colander in a bowl to cool. Press or squeeze out any excess water from the filling so that you don't end up with soggy egg rolls. 2. Make the egg rolls: Place the egg roll wrappers on a flat surface with one of the points facing towards you so they look like diamonds. Dividing the filling evenly between the eight wrappers, spoon the mixture onto the centre of the egg roll wrappers. Spread the filling across the centre of the wrappers from the left corner to the right corner but leave 2 inches from each corner empty. Brush the empty sides of the wrapper with a little water. Fold the bottom corner of the wrapper tightly up over the filling, trying to avoid making any air pockets. Fold the left corner in toward the centre and then the right corner toward the centre. It should now look like an envelope. Tightly roll the egg roll from the bottom to the top open corner. Press to seal the egg roll together, brushing with a little extra water if need be. Repeat this technique with all 8 egg rolls. 3. Preheat the air fryer to 190ºC. 4. Spray or brush all sides of the egg rolls with mixed vegetables oil. Air fry four egg rolls at a time for 10 minutes, turning them over halfway through the cooking time. 5. Serve hot with duck sauce or your favourite dipping sauce.

# Kale Chips with Tex-Mex Dip

**Prep time: 10 minutes | Cook time: 5 to 6 minutes | Serves 8**

240 ml Greek yoghurt

1 tablespoon chili powder

80 ml low-salt salsa, well drained

1 bunch curly kale

1 teaspoon olive oil

¼ teaspoon coarse sea salt

1. In a small bowl, combine the yoghurt, chili powder, and drained salsa; refrigerate. 2. Rinse the kale thoroughly, and pat dry. Remove the stems and ribs from the kale, using a sharp knife. Cut or tear the leaves into 3-inch pieces. 3. Toss the kale with the olive oil in a large bowl. 4. Air fry the kale in small batches at 200ºC until the leaves are crisp. This should take 5 to 6 minutes. Shake the basket once during cooking time. 5. As you remove the kale chips, sprinkle them with a bit of the sea salt. 6. When all of the kale chips are done, serve with the dip.

# Veggie Salmon Nachos

**Prep time: 10 minutes | Cook time: 9 to 12 minutes | Serves 6**

57 g baked no-salt sweetcorn tortilla chips

1 (142 g) baked salmon fillet, flaked

100 g canned low-salt black beans, rinsed and drained

1 red pepper, chopped

50 g grated carrot

1 jalapeño chillies pepper, minced

30 g shredded low-salt low-fat Swiss cheese

1 tomato, chopped

1. Preheat the air fryer to 180ºC. 2. In a baking pan, layer the tortilla chips. Top with the salmon, black beans, red pepper, carrot, jalapeño chillies, and Swiss cheese. 3. Bake in the air fryer for 9 to 12 minutes, or until the cheese is melted and starts to brown. 4. Top with the tomato and serve.

## Soft white cheese Stuffed Jalapeño Chillies Poppers

**Prep time: 12 minutes | Cook time: 6 to 8 minutes | Serves 10**

227 g soft white cheese, at room temperature
80 g panko breadcrumbs, divided
2 tablespoons fresh parsley,
minced
1 teaspoon chili powder
10 jalapeño chillies chillies, halved and seeded
Cooking oil spray

1. In a small bowl, whisk the soft white cheese, 40 g of panko, the parsley, and chili powder until combined. Stuff the cheese mixture into the jalapeño chillies halves. 2. Sprinkle the tops of the stuffed jalapeño chillies with the remaining 40 g of panko and press it lightly into the filling. 3. Insert the crisper plate into the basket and the basket into the unit. Preheat the unit by selecting AIR FRY, setting the temperature to 190ºC, and setting the time to 3 minutes. Select START/STOP to begin. 4. Once the unit is preheated, spray the crisper plate with cooking oil. Place the poppers into the basket. 5. Select AIR FRY, set the temperature to 190ºC, and set the time to 8 minutes. Select START/STOP to begin. 6. After 6 minutes, check the poppers. If they are softened and the cheese is melted, they are done. If not, resume cooking. 7. When the cooking is complete, serve warm.

## Rumaki

**Prep time: 30 minutes | Cook time: 10 to 12 minutes per batch | Makes about 24 rumaki**

283 g raw chicken livers
1 can sliced water chestnuts, drained
60 ml low-salt teriyaki sauce
12 slices turkey bacon

1. Cut livers into 1½-inch pieces, trimming out tough veins as you slice. 2. Place livers, water chestnuts, and teriyaki sauce in small container with lid. If needed, add another tablespoon of teriyaki sauce to make sure livers are covered. Refrigerate for 1 hour. 3. When ready to cook, cut bacon slices in half crosswise. 4. Wrap 1 piece of liver and 1 slice of water chestnut in each bacon strip. Secure with a cocktail stick. 5. When you have wrapped half of the livers, place them in the air fryer basket in a single layer. 6. Air fry at 200ºC for 10 to 12 minutes, until liver is done, and bacon is crispy. 7. While first batch cooks, wrap the remaining livers. Repeat step 6 to cook your second batch.

## Baked Spanakopita Dip

**Prep time: 10 minutes | Cook time: 15 minutes | Serves 2**

Olive oil cooking spray
3 tablespoons olive oil, divided
2 tablespoons minced white onion
2 garlic cloves, minced
100 g fresh spinach
113 g soft white cheese, softened
113 g feta cheese cheese,
divided
Zest of 1 lemon
¼ teaspoon ground nutmeg
1 teaspoon dried fresh dill weed
½ teaspoon salt
Pitta chips, carrot sticks, or sliced bread for serving (optional)

1. Preheat the air fryer to 180ºC. Coat the inside of a 6-inch ramekin or baking dish with olive oil cooking spray. 2. In a large frying pan over medium heat, heat 1 tablespoon of the olive oil. Add the onion, then cook for 1 minute. 3. Add in the garlic and cook, stirring for 1 minute more. 4. Reduce the heat to low and mix in the spinach and water. Let this cook for 2 to 3 minutes, or until the spinach has wilted. Remove the frying pan from the heat. 5. In a medium-sized bowl, combine the soft white cheese, 57 g of the feta cheese, and the remaining 2 tablespoons of olive oil, along with the lemon zest, nutmeg, fresh dill, and salt. Mix until just combined. 6. Add the mixed vegetables to the cheese base and stir until combined. 7. Pour the dip mixture into the prepared ramekin and top with the remaining 57 g of feta cheese cheese. 8. Place the dip into the air fryer basket and cook for 10 minutes, or until heated through and bubbling. 9. Serve with pitta chips, carrot sticks, or sliced bread.

## Lemony Endive in Curried Yoghurt

**Prep time: 5 minutes | Cook time: 10 minutes | Serves 6**

6 heads endive
120 ml plain and fat-free yoghurt
3 tablespoons lemon juice
1 teaspoon garlic powder
½ teaspoon curry powder
Salt and ground black pepper, to taste

1. Wash the endives and slice them in half lengthwise. 2. In a bowl, mix together the yoghurt, lemon juice, garlic powder, curry powder, salt and pepper. 3. Brush the endive halves with the marinade, coating them completely. Allow to sit for at least 30 minutes or up to 24 hours. 4. Preheat the air fryer to 160ºC. 5. Put the endives in the air fryer basket and air fry for 10 minutes. 6. Serve hot.

## Stuffed Fried Mushrooms

**Prep time: 20 minutes | Cook time: 10 to 11 minutes | Serves 10**

| | |
|---|---|
| 50 g panko breadcrumbs | 1 (227 g) package soft white |
| ½ teaspoon freshly ground | cheese, at room temperature |
| black pepper | 20 cremini or button |
| ½ teaspoon onion powder | mushrooms, stemmed |
| ½ teaspoon cayenne pepper | 1 to 2 tablespoons oil |

1. In a medium-sized bowl, whisk the breadcrumbs, black pepper, onion powder, and cayenne until blended. 2. Add the soft white cheese and mix until well blended. Fill each mushroom top with 1 teaspoon of the soft white cheese mixture 3. Preheat the air fryer to 180°C. Line the air fryer basket with a piece of baking paper paper. 4. Place the mushrooms on the baking paper and spritz with oil. 5. Cook for 5 minutes. Shake the basket and cook for 5 to 6 minutes more until the filling is firm and the mushrooms are soft.

## Air Fryer Popcorn with Garlic Salt

**Prep time: 3 minutes | Cook time: 10 minutes | Serves 2**

| | |
|---|---|
| 2 tablespoons olive oil | 1 teaspoon garlic salt |
| 60 g popcorn kernels | |

1. Preheat the air fryer to 190°C. 2. Tear a square of aluminium foil the size of the bottom of the air fryer and place into the air fryer. 3. Drizzle olive oil over the top of the foil, and then pour in the popcorn kernels. 4. Roast for 8 to 10 minutes, or until the popcorn stops popping. 5. Transfer the popcorn to a large bowl and sprinkle with garlic salt before serving.

## Fried Artichoke Hearts

**Prep time: 10 minutes | Cook time: 12 minutes | Serves 10**

| | |
|---|---|
| Oil, for spraying | 180 g panko breadcrumbs |
| 3 (397 g) cans quartered | 30 g grated Parmesan cheese |
| artichokes, drained and patted | Salt and freshly ground black |
| dry | pepper, to taste |
| 120 ml mayonnaise | |

1. Line the air fryer basket with baking paper and spray lightly with oil. 2. Place the artichokes on a plate. Put the mayonnaise and breadcrumbs in separate bowls. 3. Working one at a time, dredge each artichoke heart in the mayonnaise, then in the breadcrumbs to cover. 4. Place the artichokes in the prepared basket. You may need to work in batches, depending on the size of your air fryer. 5. Air fry at 190°C for 10 to 12 minutes, or until crispy and golden. 6. Sprinkle with the Parmesan cheese and season with salt and black pepper. Serve immediately.

## Lemony Pear Chips

**Prep time: 15 minutes | Cook time: 9 to 13 minutes | Serves 4**

| | |
|---|---|
| 2 firm Bosc or Anjou pears, cut | lemon juice |
| crosswise into ⅛-inch-thick | ½ teaspoon cinnamon powder |
| slices | ⅛ teaspoon ground cardamom |
| 1 tablespoon freshly squeezed | |

1. Preheat the air fryer to 190°C. 2. Separate the smaller stem-end pear rounds from the larger rounds with seeds. Remove the core and seeds from the larger slices. Sprinkle all slices with lemon juice, cinnamon, and cardamom. 3. Put the smaller chips into the air fryer basket. Air fry for 3 to 5 minutes, or until light golden, shaking the basket once during cooking. Remove from the air fryer. 4. Repeat with the larger slices, air frying for 6 to 8 minutes, or until light golden, shaking the basket once during cooking. 5. Remove the chips from the air fryer. Cool and serve or store in an airtight container at room temperature up for to 2 days.

## Garlic-Roasted Tomatoes and Olives

**Prep time: 5 minutes | Cook time: 20 minutes | Serves 6**

| | |
|---|---|
| 300 g cherry tomatoes | 1 tablespoon fresh basil, minced |
| 4 garlic cloves, roughly | 1 tablespoon fresh oregano, |
| chopped | minced |
| ½ red onion, roughly chopped | 2 tablespoons olive oil |
| 160 g black olives | ¼ to ½ teaspoon salt |
| 180 g green olives | |

1. Preheat the air fryer to 190°C. 2. In a large bowl, combine all of the ingredients and toss together so that the tomatoes and olives are coated well with the olive oil and herbs. 3. Pour the mixture into the air fryer basket, and roast for 10 minutes. Stir the mixture well, then continue roasting for an additional 10 minutes. 4. Remove from the air fryer, transfer to a serving bowl, and enjoy.

# Prawns Pirogues

Prep time: 15 minutes | Cook time: 4 to 5 minutes |
Serves 8

| | |
|---|---|
| 340 g small, peeled, and deveined raw prawns | 1 teaspoon dried fresh dill weed weed, crushed |
| 85 g soft white cheese, at room temperature | Salt, to taste |
| 2 tablespoons natural yoghurt | 4 small English cucumbers, each approximately 6 inches long |
| 1 teaspoon lemon juice | |

1. Pour 4 tablespoons water in bottom of air fryer drawer. 2. Place prawns in air fryer basket in single layer and air fry at 200ºC for 4 to 5 minutes, just until done. Watch carefully because prawns cooks quickly, and overcooking makes it tough. 3. Chop prawns into small pieces, no larger than ½ inch. Refrigerate while mixing the remaining ingredients. 4. With a fork, mash and whip the soft white cheese until smooth. 5. Stir in the yoghurt and beat until smooth. Stir in lemon juice, fresh dill weed, and chopped prawns. 6. Taste for seasoning. If needed, add ¼ to ½ teaspoon salt to suit your taste. 7. Store in refrigerator until serving time. 8. When ready to serve, wash and dry cucumbers and split them lengthwise. Scoop out the seeds and turn cucumbers upside down on kitchen roll to drain for 10 minutes. 9. Just before filling, wipe centres of cucumbers dry. Spoon the prawns mixture into the pirogues and cut in half crosswise. Serve immediately.

# Honey-Mustard Chicken Wings

Prep time: 10 minutes | Cook time: 24 minutes |
Serves 2

| | |
|---|---|
| 907 g chicken wings | 60 g spicy brown mustard |
| Salt and freshly ground black pepper, to taste | Pinch ground cayenne pepper |
| 2 tablespoons butter | 2 teaspoons Worcestershire sauce |
| 60 ml honey | |

1. Prepare the chicken wings by cutting off the wing tips and discarding (or freezing for chicken stock). Divide the chicken drumettes from the chicken wingettes by cutting through the joint. Place the chicken wing pieces in a large bowl. 2. Preheat the air fryer to 200ºC. 3. Season the wings with salt and freshly ground black pepper and air fry the wings in two batches for 10 minutes per batch, shaking the basket halfway through the cooking process. 4. While the wings are air frying, combine the remaining ingredients in a small saucepan over low heat. 5. When both batches are done, toss all the wings with the honey-mustard sauce and toss them all back into the basket for another 4 minutes to heat through and finish cooking. Give the basket a good shake part way through the cooking process to redistribute the wings. Remove the wings from the air fryer and serve.

# Peppery Chicken Meatballs

Prep time: 5 minutes | Cook time: 13 to 20 minutes |
Makes 16 meatballs

| | |
|---|---|
| 2 teaspoons olive oil | 1 egg white |
| 35 g minced onion | ½ teaspoon dried thyme |
| 35 g minced red pepper | 230 g minced chicken breast |
| 2 vanilla wafers, crushed | |

1. Preheat the air fryer to 188ºC. 2. In a baking pan, mix the olive oil, onion, and red pepper. Put the pan in the air fryer. Air fry for 3 to 5 minutes, or until the mixed vegetables are tender. 3. In a medium-sized bowl, mix the cooked mixed vegetables, crushed wafers, egg white, and thyme until well combined 4. Mix in the chicken, gently but thoroughly, until everything is combined. 5. Form the mixture into 16 meatballs and place them in the air fryer basket. Air fry for 10 to 15 minutes, or until the meatballs reach an internal temperature of 70ºC on a meat thermometer. 6. Serve immediately.

# Mozzarella Cheese Arancini

Prep time: 5 minutes | Cook time: 8 to 11 minutes |
Makes 16 arancini

| | |
|---|---|
| 250 g cooked rice, cooled | 2 tablespoons minced fresh basil |
| 2 eggs, beaten | |
| 90 g panko breadcrumbs, divided | 16 ¾-inch cubes mozzarella cheese cheese |
| 45 g grated Parmesan cheese | 2 tablespoons olive oil |

1. Preheat the air fryer to 200ºC. 2. In a medium-sized bowl, combine the rice, eggs, 120 ml of the breadcrumbs, Parmesan cheese, and basil. Form this mixture into 16 1½-inch balls. 3. Poke a hole in each of the balls with your finger and insert a mozzarella cheese cube. Form the rice mixture firmly around the cheese. 4. On a shallow plate, combine the remaining 100 g of the breadcrumbs with the olive oil and mix well. Roll the rice balls in the breadcrumbs to coat. 5. Air fry the arancini in batches for 8 to 11 minutes or until golden. 6. Serve hot.

# Chapter 8 Vegetables and Sides

# Chapter 8 Vegetables and Sides

## Courgette Fritters

**Prep time: 10 minutes | Cook time: 10 minutes |**
**Serves 4**

| | |
|---|---|
| 2 courgette, grated (about 450 g) | ¼ teaspoon dried thyme |
| | ¼ teaspoon ground turmeric |
| 1 teaspoon salt | ¼ teaspoon freshly ground |
| 25 g almond flour | black pepper |
| 20 g grated Parmesan cheese | 1 tablespoon olive oil |
| 1 large egg | ½ lemon, sliced into wedges |

1. Preheat the air fryer to 200ºC. Cut a piece of parchment paper to fit slightly smaller than the bottom of the air fryer. 2. Place the courgette in a large colander and sprinkle with the salt. Let sit for 5 to 10 minutes. Squeeze as much liquid as you can from the courgette and place in a large mixing bowl. Add the almond flour, Parmesan, egg, thyme, turmeric, and black pepper. Stir gently until thoroughly combined. 3. Shape the mixture into 8 patties and arrange on the parchment paper. Brush lightly with the olive oil. Pausing halfway through the cooking time to turn the patties, air fry for 10 minutes until golden brown. Serve warm with the lemon wedges.

## Gorgonzola Mushrooms with Horseradish Mayo

**Prep time: 15 minutes | Cook time: 10 minutes |**
**Serves 5**

| | |
|---|---|
| 60 g bread crumbs | 20 medium mushrooms, stems |
| 2 cloves garlic, pressed | removed |
| 2 tablespoons chopped fresh coriander | 55 g grated Gorgonzola cheese |
| | 55 g low-fat mayonnaise |
| ⅓ teaspoon coarse sea salt | 1 teaspoon prepared |
| ½ teaspoon crushed red pepper flakes | horseradish, well-drained |
| | 1 tablespoon finely chopped |
| 1½ tablespoons olive oil | fresh parsley |

1. Preheat the air fryer to 190ºC. 2. Combine the bread crumbs together with the garlic, coriander, salt, red pepper, and olive oil. 3. Take equal-sized amounts of the bread crumb mixture and use them to stuff the mushroom caps. Add the grated Gorgonzola on top of each. 4. Put the mushrooms in a baking pan and transfer to the air fryer. 5. Air fry for 10 minutes, ensuring the stuffing is warm throughout. 6. In the meantime, prepare the horseradish mayo. Mix the mayonnaise, horseradish and parsley. 7. When the mushrooms are ready, serve with the mayo.

## Buffalo Cauliflower with Blue Cheese

**Prep time: 15 minutes | Cook time: 5 to 7 minutes**
**per batch | Serves 6**

| | |
|---|---|
| 1 large head cauliflower, rinsed and separated into small florets | 190 g nonfat Greek yogurt |
| | 60 g buttermilk |
| 1 tablespoon extra-virgin olive oil | ½ teaspoon hot sauce |
| | 1 celery stalk, chopped |
| ½ teaspoon garlic powder | 2 tablespoons crumbled blue |
| Cooking oil spray | cheese |
| 80 ml hot wing sauce | |

1. Insert the crisper plate into the basket and the basket into the unit. Preheat the unit by selecting AIR FRY, setting the temperature to190ºC, and setting the time to 3 minutes. Select START/STOP to begin. 2. In a large bowl, toss together the cauliflower florets and olive oil. Sprinkle with the garlic powder and toss again to coat. 3. Once the unit is preheated, spray the crisper plate with cooking oil. Put half the cauliflower into the basket. 4. Select AIR FRY, set the temperature to190ºC, and set the time to 7 minutes. Select START/ STOP to begin. 5. After 3 minutes, remove the basket and shake the cauliflower. Reinsert the basket to resume cooking. After 2 minutes, check the cauliflower. It is done when it is browned. If not, resume cooking. 6. When the cooking is complete, transfer the cauliflower to a serving bowl and toss with half the hot wing sauce. 7. Repeat steps 4, 5, and 6 with the remaining cauliflower and hot wing sauce. 8. In a small bowl, stir together the yogurt, buttermilk, hot sauce, celery, and blue cheese. Drizzle the sauce over the finished cauliflower and serve.

# Crispy Courgette Sticks

**Prep time: 5 minutes | Cook time: 14 minutes |**
**Serves 4**

2 small courgette, cut into
2-inch × ½-inch sticks
3 tablespoons chickpea flour
2 teaspoons arrowroot (or
cornflour)
½ teaspoon garlic granules

¼ teaspoon sea salt
⅛ teaspoon freshly ground
black pepper
1 tablespoon water
Cooking spray

1. Preheat the air fryer to 200ºC. 2. Combine the courgette sticks with the chickpea flour, arrowroot, garlic granules, salt, and pepper in a medium bowl and toss to coat. Add the water and stir to mix well. 3. Spritz the air fryer basket with cooking spray and spread out the courgette sticks in the basket. Mist the courgette sticks with cooking spray. 4. Air fry for 14 minutes, shaking the basket halfway through, or until the courgette sticks are crispy and nicely browned. 5. Serve warm.

# Saltine Wax Beans

**Prep time: 10 minutes | Cook time: 7 minutes |**
**Serves 4**

60 g flour
1 teaspoon smoky chipotle
powder
½ teaspoon ground black
pepper

1 teaspoon sea salt flakes
2 eggs, beaten
55 g crushed cream crackers
285 g wax beans
Cooking spray

1. Preheat the air fryer to 180ºC. 2. Combine the flour, chipotle powder, black pepper, and salt in a bowl. Put the eggs in a second bowl. Put the crushed cream crackers in a third bowl. 3. Wash the beans with cold water and discard any tough strings. 4. Coat the beans with the flour mixture, before dipping them into the beaten egg. Cover them with the crushed cream crackers. 5. Spritz the beans with cooking spray. 6. Air fry for 4 minutes. Give the air fryer basket a good shake and continue to air fry for 3 minutes. Serve hot.

# Asian Tofu Salad

**Prep time: 25 minutes | Cook time: 15 minutes |**
**Serves 2**

Tofu:
1 tablespoon soy sauce
1 tablespoon vegetable oil
1 teaspoon minced fresh ginger
1 teaspoon minced garlic
230 g extra-firm tofu, drained
and cubed
Salad:
60 ml rice vinegar

1 tablespoon sugar
1 teaspoon salt
1 teaspoon black pepper
25 g sliced spring onions
120 g julienned cucumber
50 g julienned red onion
130 g julienned carrots
6 butter lettuce leaves

1. For the tofu: In a small bowl, whisk together the soy sauce, vegetable oil, ginger, and garlic. Add the tofu and mix gently. Let stand at room temperature for 10 minutes. 2. Arrange the tofu in a single layer in the air fryer basket. Set the air fryer to 200ºC for 15 minutes, shaking halfway through the cooking time. 3. Meanwhile, for the salad: In a large bowl, whisk together the vinegar, sugar, salt, pepper, and spring onions. Add the cucumber, onion, and carrots and toss to combine. Set aside to marinate while the tofu cooks. 4. To serve, arrange three lettuce leaves on each of two plates. Pile the marinated vegetables (and marinade) on the lettuce. Divide the tofu between the plates and serve.

# Garlic-Parmesan Crispy Baby Potatoes

**Prep time: 10 minutes | Cook time: 15 minutes |**
**Serves 4**

Oil, for spraying
450 g baby potatoes
45 g grated Parmesan cheese,
divided
3 tablespoons olive oil
2 teaspoons garlic powder
½ teaspoon onion powder

½ teaspoon salt
¼ teaspoon freshly ground
black pepper
¼ teaspoon paprika
2 tablespoons chopped fresh
parsley, for garnish

1. Line the air fryer basket with parchment and spray lightly with oil. 2. Rinse the potatoes, pat dry with paper towels, and place in a large bowl. 3. In a small bowl, mix together 45 g of Parmesan cheese, the olive oil, garlic, onion powder, salt, black pepper, and paprika. Pour the mixture over the potatoes and toss to coat. 4. Transfer the potatoes to the prepared basket and spread them out in an even layer, taking care to keep them from touching. You may need to work in batches, depending on the size of your air fryer. 5. Air fry at 200ºC for 15 minutes, stirring after 7 to 8 minutes, or until easily pierced with a fork. Continue to cook for another 1 to 2 minutes, if needed. 6. Sprinkle with the parsley and the remaining Parmesan cheese and serve.

## Butternut Squash Croquettes

**Prep time: 5 minutes | Cook time: 17 minutes |**
**Serves 4**

⅓ butternut squash, peeled and grated

40 g plain flour

2 eggs, whisked

4 cloves garlic, minced

1½ tablespoons olive oil

1 teaspoon fine sea salt

⅓ teaspoon freshly ground black pepper, or more to taste

⅓ teaspoon dried sage

A pinch of ground allspice

1. Preheat the air fryer to 170ºC. Line the air fryer basket with parchment paper. 2. In a mixing bowl, stir together all the ingredients until well combined. 3. Make the squash croquettes: Use a small cookie scoop to drop tablespoonfuls of the squash mixture onto a lightly floured surface and shape into balls with your hands. Transfer them to the air fryer basket. 4. Air fry for 17 minutes until the squash croquettes are golden brown. 5. Remove from the basket to a plate and serve warm.

## Marinara Pepperoni Mushroom Pizza

**Prep time: 5 minutes | Cook time: 18 minutes |**
**Serves 4**

4 large portobello mushrooms, stems removed

4 teaspoons olive oil

225 g marinara sauce

225 g shredded Mozzarella cheese

10 slices sugar-free pepperoni

1. Preheat the air fryer to 190ºC. 2. Brush each mushroom cap with the olive oil, one teaspoon for each cap. 3. Put on a baking sheet and bake, stem-side down, for 8 minutes. 4. Take out of the air fryer and divide the marinara sauce, Mozzarella cheese and pepperoni evenly among the caps. 5. Air fry for another 10 minutes until browned. 6. Serve hot.

## Garlic Herb Radishes

**Prep time: 10 minutes | Cook time: 10 minutes |**
**Serves 4**

450 g radishes

2 tablespoons unsalted butter, melted

½ teaspoon garlic powder

½ teaspoon dried parsley

¼ teaspoon dried oregano

¼ teaspoon ground black pepper

1. Remove roots from radishes and cut into quarters. 2. In a small bowl, add butter and seasonings. Toss the radishes in the herb butter and place into the air fryer basket. 3. Adjust the temperature to 180ºC and set the timer for 10 minutes. 4. Halfway through the cooking time, toss the radishes in the air fryer basket. Continue cooking until edges begin to turn brown. 5. Serve warm.

## Easy Rosemary Green Beans

**Prep time: 5 minutes | Cook time: 5 minutes | Serves 1**

1 tablespoon butter, melted

2 tablespoons rosemary

½ teaspoon salt

3 cloves garlic, minced

95 g chopped green beans

1. Preheat the air fryer to 200ºC. 2. Combine the melted butter with the rosemary, salt, and minced garlic. Toss in the green beans, coating them well. 3. Air fry for 5 minutes. 4. Serve immediately.

## Roasted Grape Tomatoes and Asparagus

**Prep time: 5 minutes | Cook time: 12 minutes |**
**Serves 6**

400 g grape tomatoes

1 bunch asparagus, trimmed

2 tablespoons olive oil

3 garlic cloves, minced

½ teaspoon coarse sea salt

1. Preheat the air fryer to 190ºC. 2. In a large bowl, combine all of the ingredients, tossing until the vegetables are well coated with oil. 3. Pour the vegetable mixture into the air fryer basket and spread into a single layer, then roast for 12 minutes.

## Curried Fruit

**Prep time: 10 minutes | Cook time: 20 minutes |**
**Serves 6 to 8**

210 g cubed fresh pineapple

200 g cubed fresh pear (firm, not overly ripe)

230 g frozen peaches, thawed

425 g can dark, sweet, pitted cherries with juice

2 tablespoons brown sugar

1 teaspoon curry powder

1. Combine all ingredients in large bowl. Stir gently to mix in the sugar and curry. 2. Pour into a baking pan and bake at 180ºC for 10 minutes. 3. Stir fruit and cook 10 more minutes. 4. Serve hot.

## Roasted Potatoes and Asparagus

**Prep time: 5 minutes | Cook time: 23 minutes |**
**Serves 4**

| | |
|---|---|
| 4 medium potatoes | 1 tablespoon wholegrain |
| 1 bunch asparagus | mustard |
| 75 g cottage cheese | Salt and pepper, to taste |
| 80 g low-fat crème fraiche | Cooking spray |

1. Preheat the air fryer to 200ºC. Spritz the air fryer basket with cooking spray. 2. Place the potatoes in the basket. Air fry the potatoes for 20 minutes. 3. Boil the asparagus in salted water for 3 minutes. 4. Remove the potatoes and mash them with rest of ingredients. Sprinkle with salt and pepper. 5. Serve immediately.

## Mushrooms with Goat Cheese

**Prep time: 10 minutes | Cook time: 10 minutes |**
**Serves 4**

| | |
|---|---|
| 3 tablespoons vegetable oil | ½ teaspoon black pepper |
| 450 g mixed mushrooms, | 110 g goat cheese, diced |
| trimmed and sliced | 2 teaspoons chopped fresh |
| 1 clove garlic, minced | thyme leaves (optional) |
| ¼ teaspoon dried thyme | |

1. In a baking pan, combine the oil, mushrooms, garlic, dried thyme, and pepper. Stir in the goat cheese. Place the pan in the air fryer basket. Set the air fryer to 200ºC for 10 minutes, stirring halfway through the cooking time. 2. Sprinkle with fresh thyme, if desired.

## Mashed Sweet Potato Tots

**Prep time: 10 minutes | Cook time: 12 to 13 minutes**
**per batch | Makes 18 to 24 tots**

| | |
|---|---|
| 210 g cooked mashed sweet | 2 tablespoons chopped pecans |
| potatoes | 1½ teaspoons honey |
| 1 egg white, beaten | Salt, to taste |
| ⅛ teaspoon ground cinnamon | 50 g panko bread crumbs |
| 1 dash nutmeg | Oil for misting or cooking spray |

1. Preheat the air fryer to 200ºC. 2. In a large bowl, mix together the potatoes, egg white, cinnamon, nutmeg, pecans, honey, and salt to taste. 3. Place panko crumbs on a sheet of wax paper. 4. For each tot, use about 2 teaspoons of sweet potato mixture. To shape, drop the measure of potato mixture onto panko crumbs and push crumbs up and around potatoes to coat edges. Then turn tot over to coat other side with crumbs. 5. Mist tots with oil or cooking spray and place in air fryer basket in single layer. 6. Air fry at 200ºC for 12 to 13 minutes, until browned and crispy. 7. Repeat steps 5 and 6 to cook remaining tots.

## "Faux-Tato" Hash

**Prep time: 10 minutes | Cook time: 12 minutes |**
**Serves 4**

| | |
|---|---|
| 450 g radishes, ends removed, | 2 tablespoons salted butter, |
| quartered | melted |
| ¼ medium yellow onion, peeled | ½ teaspoon garlic powder |
| and diced | ¼ teaspoon ground black |
| ½ medium green pepper, seeded | pepper |
| and chopped | |

1. In a large bowl, combine radishes, onion, and bell pepper. Toss with butter. 2. Sprinkle garlic powder and black pepper over mixture in bowl, then spoon into ungreased air fryer basket. 3. Adjust the temperature to 160ºC and air fry for 12 minutes. Shake basket halfway through cooking. Radishes will be tender when done. Serve warm.

## Golden Pickles

**Prep time: 10 minutes | Cook time: 15 minutes |**
**Serves 4**

| | |
|---|---|
| 14 dill pickles, sliced | tablespoons water |
| 30 g flour | 6 tablespoons panko bread |
| ⅛ teaspoon baking powder | crumbs |
| Pinch of salt | ½ teaspoon paprika |
| 2 tablespoons cornflour plus 3 | Cooking spray |

1. Preheat the air fryer to 200ºC. 2. Drain any excess moisture out of the dill pickles on a paper towel. 3. In a bowl, combine the flour, baking powder and salt. 4. Throw in the cornflour and water mixture and combine well with a whisk. 5. Put the panko bread crumbs in a shallow dish along with the paprika. Mix thoroughly. 6. Dip the pickles in the flour batter, before coating in the bread crumbs. Spritz all the pickles with the cooking spray. 7. Transfer to the air fryer basket and air fry for 15 minutes, or until golden brown. 8. Serve immediately.

## Cheddar Broccoli with Bacon

### Prep time: 10 minutes | Cook time: 10 minutes | Serves 2

| | |
|---|---|
| 215 g fresh broccoli florets | 4 slices sugar-free bacon, |
| 1 tablespoon coconut oil | cooked and crumbled |
| 115 g shredded sharp Cheddar | 1 spring onion, sliced on the |
| cheese | bias |
| 60 g full-fat sour cream | |

1. Place broccoli into the air fryer basket and drizzle it with coconut oil. 2. Adjust the temperature to 180°C and set the timer for 10 minutes. 3. Toss the basket two or three times during cooking to avoid burned spots. 4. When broccoli begins to crisp at ends, remove from fryer. Top with shredded cheese, sour cream, and crumbled bacon and garnish with spring onion slices.

## Flatbread

### Prep time: 5 minutes | Cook time: 7 minutes | Serves 2

| | |
|---|---|
| 225 g shredded Mozzarella | almond flour |
| cheese | 30 g full-fat cream cheese, |
| 25 g blanched finely ground | softened |

1. In a large microwave-safe bowl, melt Mozzarella in the microwave for 30 seconds. Stir in almond flour until smooth and then add cream cheese. Continue mixing until dough forms, gently kneading it with wet hands if necessary. 2. Divide the dough into two pieces and roll out to ¼-inch thickness between two pieces of parchment. Cut another piece of parchment to fit your air fryer basket. 3. Place a piece of flatbread onto your parchment and into the air fryer, working in two batches if needed. 4. Adjust the temperature to 160°C and air fry for 7 minutes. 5. Halfway through the cooking time flip the flatbread. Serve warm.

## Fried Asparagus

### Prep time: 5 minutes | Cook time: 12 minutes | Serves 4

| | |
|---|---|
| 1 tablespoon olive oil | ¼ teaspoon ground black |
| 450 g asparagus spears, ends | pepper |
| trimmed | 1 tablespoon salted butter, |
| ¼ teaspoon salt | melted |

1. In a large bowl, drizzle olive oil over asparagus spears and sprinkle with salt and pepper. 2. Place spears into ungreased air fryer basket. Adjust the temperature to 190°C and set the timer for 12 minutes, shaking the basket halfway through cooking. Asparagus will be lightly browned and tender when done. 3. Transfer to a large dish and drizzle with butter. Serve warm.

## Mexican Corn in a Cup

### Prep time: 5 minutes | Cook time: 10 minutes | Serves 4

| | |
|---|---|
| 650 g frozen corn kernels (do | 2 tablespoons fresh lemon or |
| not thaw) | lime juice |
| Vegetable oil spray | 1 teaspoon chili powder |
| 2 tablespoons butter | Chopped fresh green onion |
| 60 g sour cream | (optional) |
| 60 g mayonnaise | Chopped fresh coriander |
| 20 g grated Parmesan cheese (or | (optional) |
| feta, cotija, or queso fresco) | |

1. Place the corn in the bottom of the air fryer basket and spray with vegetable oil spray. Set the air fryer to 180°C for 10 minutes. 2. Transfer the corn to a serving bowl. Add the butter and stir until melted. Add the sour cream, mayonnaise, cheese, lemon juice, and chili powder; stir until well combined. Serve immediately with green onion and coriander (if using).

## Roasted Salsa

### Prep time: 15 minutes | Cook time: 30 minutes | Makes 500 g

| | |
|---|---|
| 2 large San Marzano tomatoes, | 2 cloves garlic, peeled and |
| cored and cut into large chunks | diced |
| ½ medium white onion, peeled | ½ teaspoon salt |
| and large-diced | 1 tablespoon coconut oil |
| ½ medium jalapeño, seeded and | 65 g fresh lime juice |
| large-diced | |

1. Place tomatoes, onion, and jalapeño into an ungreased round nonstick baking dish. Add garlic, then sprinkle with salt and drizzle with coconut oil. 2. Place dish into air fryer basket. Adjust the temperature to 150°C and bake for 30 minutes. Vegetables will be dark brown around the edges and tender when done. 3. Pour mixture into a food processor or blender. Add lime juice. Process on low speed 30 seconds until only a few chunks remain. 4. Transfer salsa to a sealable container and refrigerate at least 1 hour. Serve chilled.

# Scalloped Potatoes

**Prep time: 5 minutes | Cook time: 20 minutes | Serves 4**

440 g sliced frozen potatoes, thawed

3 cloves garlic, minced

Pinch salt

Freshly ground black pepper, to taste

180 g double cream

1. Preheat the air fryer to 190°C. 2. Toss the potatoes with the garlic, salt, and black pepper in a baking pan until evenly coated. Pour the double cream over the top. 3. Place the baking pan in the air fryer basket and bake for 15 minutes, or until the potatoes are tender and top is golden brown. Check for doneness and bake for another 5 minutes as needed. 4. Serve hot.

# Citrus Sweet Potatoes and Carrots

**Prep time: 5 minutes | Cook time: 20 to 25 minutes | Serves 4**

2 large carrots, cut into 1-inch chunks

1 medium sweet potato, peeled and cut into 1-inch cubes

25 g chopped onion

2 garlic cloves, minced

2 tablespoons honey

1 tablespoon freshly squeezed orange juice

2 teaspoons butter, melted

1. Insert the crisper plate into the basket and the basket into the unit. Preheat the unit by selecting AIR ROAST, setting the temperature to 200°C, and setting the time to 3 minutes. Select START/STOP to begin. 2. In a 6-by-2-inch round pan, toss together the carrots, sweet potato, onion, garlic, honey, orange juice, and melted butter to coat. 3. Once the unit is preheated, place the pan into the basket. 4. Select AIR ROAST, set the temperature to 200°C, and set the time to 25 minutes. Select START/STOP to begin. 5. After 15 minutes, remove the basket and shake the vegetables. Reinsert the basket to resume cooking. After 5 minutes, if the vegetables are tender and glazed, they are done. If not, resume cooking. 6. When the cooking is complete, serve immediately.

# Chapter 9 Vegetarian Mains

# Chapter 9 Vegetarian Mains

## Spinach-Artichoke Stuffed Mushrooms

**Prep time: 10 minutes | Cook time: 10 to 14 minutes | Serves 4**

2 tablespoons olive oil
4 large portobello mushrooms, stems removed and gills scraped out
½ teaspoon salt
¼ teaspoon freshly ground pepper
110 g goat cheese, crumbled
120 g chopped marinated artichoke hearts
235 g frozen spinach, thawed and squeezed dry
120 g grated Parmesan cheese
2 tablespoons chopped fresh parsley

1. Preheat the air fryer to 200°C. 2.Rub the olive oil over the portobello mushrooms until thoroughly coated. 3.Sprinkle both sides with the salt and black pepper. 4.Place top-side down on a clean work surface. 5.In a small bowl, combine the goat cheese, artichoke hearts, and spinach. 6.Mash with the back of a fork until thoroughly combined. 7.Divide the cheese mixture among the mushrooms and sprinkle with the Parmesan cheese. 8.Air fry for 10 to 14 minutes until the mushrooms are tender and the cheese has begun to brown. 9.Top with the fresh parsley just before serving.

## Three-Cheese Courgette Boats

**Prep time: 15 minutes | Cook time: 20 minutes | Serves 2**

2 medium courgette
1 tablespoon avocado oil
60 ml low-carb, no-sugar-added pasta sauce
60 g full-fat ricotta cheese
60 g shredded Mozzarella cheese
¼ teaspoon dried oregano
¼ teaspoon garlic powder
½ teaspoon dried parsley
2 tablespoons grated vegetarian Parmesan cheese

1. Cut off 1 inch from the top and bottom of each courgette. 2.Slice courgette in half lengthwise and use a spoon to scoop out a bit of the inside, making room for filling. 3.Brush with oil and spoon 2 tablespoons pasta sauce into each shell. In a medium bowl, mix ricotta, Mozzarella, oregano, garlic powder, and parsley. 4.Spoon the mixture into each courgette shell. Place stuffed courgette shells into the air fryer basket. 5.Adjust the temperature to 180°C and air fry for 20 minutes. To remove from the basket, use tongs or a spatula and carefully lift out. 6.Top with Parmesan. 7.Serve immediately.

## Cauliflower Rice-Stuffed Peppers

**Prep time: 10 minutes | Cook time: 15 minutes | Serves 4**

475 g uncooked cauliflower rice
180 g drained canned petite diced tomatoes
2 tablespoons olive oil
235 g shredded Mozzarella cheese
¼ teaspoon salt
¼ teaspoon ground black pepper
4 medium green peppers, tops removed, seeded

1. In a large bowl, mix all ingredients except peppers. 2.Scoop mixture evenly into peppers. 3.Place peppers into ungreased air fryer basket. 4.Adjust the temperature to 180°C and air fry for 15 minutes. 5.Peppers will be tender, and cheese will be melted when done. 6.Serve warm.

## Air Fryer Veggies with Halloumi

**Prep time: 5 minutes | Cook time: 14 minutes | Serves 2**

2 courgettes, cut into even chunks
1 large aubergine, peeled, cut into chunks
1 large carrot, cut into chunks
170 g halloumi cheese, cubed
2 teaspoons olive oil
Salt and black pepper, to taste
1 teaspoon dried mixed herbs

1. Preheat the air fryer to 170°C. 2.Combine the courgettes, aubergine, carrot, cheese, olive oil, salt, and pepper in a large bowl and toss to coat well. 3.Spread the mixture evenly in the air fryer basket and air fry for 14 minutes until crispy and golden, shaking the basket once during cooking. 4.Serve topped with mixed herbs.

# Basmati Risotto

**Prep time: 10 minutes | Cook time: 30 minutes |**

**Serves 2**

| | |
|---|---|
| 1 onion, diced | 1 clove garlic, minced |
| 1 small carrot, diced | 180 g long-grain basmati rice |
| 475 ml vegetable broth, boiling | 1 tablespoon olive oil |
| 120 g grated Cheddar cheese | 1 tablespoon unsalted butter |

1. Preheat the air fryer to 200ºC. 2.Grease a baking tin with oil and stir in the butter, garlic, carrot, and onion. 3.Put the tin in the air fryer and bake for 4 minutes. 4.Pour in the rice and bake for a further 4 minutes, stirring three times throughout the baking time. 5.Turn the temperature down to 160ºC. 6.Add the vegetable broth and give the dish a gentle stir. 7.Bake for 22 minutes, leaving the air fryer uncovered. 8.Pour in the cheese, stir once more and serve.

# Quiche-Stuffed Peppers

**Prep time: 5 minutes | Cook time: 15 minutes |**

**Serves 2**

| | |
|---|---|
| 2 medium green peppers | 120 g chopped broccoli |
| 3 large eggs | 120 g shredded medium |
| 60 g full-fat ricotta cheese | Cheddar cheese |
| 60 g diced brown onion | |

1. Cut the tops off of the peppers and remove the seeds and white membranes with a small knife. 2.In a medium bowl, whisk eggs and ricotta. 3.Add onion and broccoli. 4.Pour the egg and vegetable mixture evenly into each pepper. 5.Top with Cheddar. 6.Place peppers into a 1 L round baking dish and place into the air fryer basket. 7.Adjust the temperature to 180ºC and bake for 15 minutes. 8.Eggs will be mostly firm and peppers tender when fully cooked. 9.Serve immediately.

# Cheese Stuffed Courgette

**Prep time: 20 minutes | Cook time: 8 minutes |**

**Serves 4**

| | |
|---|---|
| 1 large courgette, cut into four pieces | chopped |
| 2 tablespoons olive oil | 1 heaping tablespoon fresh parsley, roughly chopped |
| 235 g Ricotta cheese, room temperature | 1 heaping tablespoon coriander, minced |
| 2 tablespoons spring onions, | 60 g Cheddar cheese, preferably |

freshly grated

1 teaspoon celery seeds

½ teaspoon salt

½ teaspoon garlic pepper

1. Cook your courgette in the air fryer basket for approximately 10 minutes at 180ºC. 2.Check for doneness and cook for 2-3 minutes longer if needed. 3.Meanwhile, make the stuffing by mixing the other items. 4.When your courgette is thoroughly cooked, open them up. 5.Divide the stuffing among all courgette pieces and bake an additional 5 minutes.

# Crispy Fried Okra with Chilli

**Prep time: 5 minutes | Cook time: 10 minutes |**

**Serves 4**

| | |
|---|---|
| 3 tablespoons sour cream | Salt and black pepper, to taste |
| 2 tablespoons flour | 450 g okra, halved |
| 2 tablespoons semolina | Cooking spray |
| ½ teaspoon red chilli powder | |

1. Preheat the air fryer to 200ºC. 2.Spray the air fryer basket with cooking spray. 3.In a shallow bowl, place the sour cream. 4.In another shallow bowl, thoroughly combine the flour, semolina, red chilli powder, salt, and pepper. 5.Dredge the okra in the sour cream, then roll in the flour mixture until evenly coated. 6.Arrange the okra in the air fryer basket and air fry for 10 minutes, flipping the okra halfway through, or until golden brown and crispy. 7.Cool for 5 minutes before serving.

# Vegetable Burgers

**Prep time: 10 minutes | Cook time: 12 minutes |**

**Serves 4**

| | |
|---|---|
| 227 g cremini or chestnut mushrooms | onion |
| 2 large egg yolks | 1 clove garlic, peeled and finely minced |
| ½ medium courgette, trimmed and chopped | ½ teaspoon salt |
| 60 g peeled and chopped brown | ¼ teaspoon ground black pepper |

1. Place all ingredients into a food processor and pulse twenty times until finely chopped and combined. 2.Separate mixture into four equal sections and press each into a burger shape. 3.Place burgers into ungreased air fryer basket. 4.Adjust the temperature to 190ºC and air fry for 12 minutes, turning burgers halfway through cooking. 5.Burgers will be browned and firm when done. 6.Place burgers on a large plate and let cool 5 minutes before serving.

# Parmesan Artichokes

**Prep time: 10 minutes | Cook time: 10 minutes | Serves 4**

2 medium artichokes, trimmed and quartered, centre removed

2 tablespoons coconut oil

1 large egg, beaten

120 g grated vegetarian Parmesan cheese

60 g blanched finely ground almond flour

½ teaspoon crushed red pepper flakes

1. In a large bowl, toss artichokes in coconut oil and then dip each piece into the egg. 2.Mix the Parmesan and almond flour in a large bowl. 3.Add artichoke pieces and toss to cover as completely as possible, sprinkle with pepper flakes. 4.Place into the air fryer basket. 5.Adjust the temperature to 200°C and air fry for 10 minutes. 6.Toss the basket two times during cooking. 7.Serve warm.

# Chapter 10 Desserts

# Chapter 10 Desserts

## Spiced Apple Cake

**Prep time: 15 minutes | Cook time: 30 minutes | Serves 6**

| | |
|---|---|
| Vegetable oil | 1 tablespoon apple pie spice |
| 2 diced & peeled Gala apples | ½ teaspoon ground ginger |
| 1 tablespoon fresh lemon juice | ¼ teaspoon ground cardamom |
| 55 g unsalted butter, softened | ¼ teaspoon ground nutmeg |
| 50 g granulated sugar | ½ teaspoon kosher, or coarse |
| 2 large eggs | sea salt |
| 80 g All-purpose flour | 60 ml whole milk |
| 1½ teaspoons baking powder | Icing sugar, for dusting |

1. Grease a 0.7-liter Bundt, or tube pan with oil; set aside. 2. In a medium bowl, toss the apples with the lemon juice until well coated; set aside. 3. In a large bowl, combine the butter and sugar. Beat with an electric hand mixer on medium speed until the sugar has dissolved. Add the eggs and beat until fluffy. Add the flour, baking powder, apple pie spice, ginger, cardamom, nutmeg, salt, and milk. Mix until the batter is thick but pourable. 4. Pour the batter into the prepared pan. Top batter evenly with the apple mixture. Place the pan in the air fryer basket. Set the air fryer to 180°C and cook for 30 minutes, or until a toothpick inserted in the center of the cake comes out clean. Close the air fryer and let the cake rest for 10 minutes. Turn the cake out onto a wire rack and cool completely. 5. Right before serving, dust the cake with icing sugar.

## Pumpkin Cookie with Cream Cheese Frosting

**Prep time: 10 minutes | Cook time: 7 minutes | Serves 6**

| | |
|---|---|
| 25 g blanched finely ground almond flour | ½ teaspoon unflavoured gelatin |
| 25 g powdered sweetener, divided | ½ teaspoon baking powder |
| 2 tablespoons butter, softened | ½ teaspoon vanilla extract |
| 1 large egg | ½ teaspoon pumpkin pie spice |
| | 2 tablespoons pure pumpkin purée |

| | |
|---|---|
| ½ teaspoon ground cinnamon, divided | chocolate chips |
| 40 g low-carb, sugar-free | 85 g full-fat cream cheese, softened |

1. In a large bowl, mix almond flour and 25 gsweetener. Stir in butter, egg, and gelatin until combined. 2. Stir in baking powder, vanilla, pumpkin pie spice, pumpkin purée, and ¼ teaspoon cinnamon, then fold in chocolate chips. 3. Pour batter into a round baking pan. Place pan into the air fryer basket. 4. Adjust the temperature to 150°C and bake for 7 minutes. 5. When fully cooked, the top will be golden brown, and a toothpick inserted in center will come out clean. Let cool at least 20 minutes. 6. To make the frosting: mix cream cheese, remaining ¼ teaspoon cinnamon, and remaining 25 g sweetener in a large bowl. Using an electric mixer, beat until it becomes fluffy. Spread onto the cooled cookie. Garnish with additional cinnamon if desired.

## Blackberry Peach Cobbler with Vanilla

**Prep time: 10 minutes | Cook time: 20 minutes | Serves 4**

| | |
|---|---|
| Filling: | 1 tablespoon maple syrup |
| 170 g blackberries | 1 teaspoon vanilla |
| 250 g chopped peaches, cut into ½-inch thick slices | 3 tablespoons coconut sugar |
| | 40 g rolled oats |
| 2 teaspoons arrowroot or cornflour | 25 g whole-wheat pastry, or All-purpose flour |
| 2 tablespoons coconut sugar | 1 teaspoon cinnamon |
| 1 teaspoon lemon juice | ¼ teaspoon nutmeg |
| Topping: | ⅛ teaspoon sea salt |
| 2 tablespoons sunflower oil | |

Make the Filling: 1. Combine the blackberries, peaches, arrowroot, coconut sugar, and lemon juice in a baking pan. 2. Using a rubber spatula, stir until well incorporated. Set aside. Make the Topping: 3. Preheat the air fryer to 160°C 4. Combine the oil, maple syrup, and vanilla in a mixing bowl and stir well. Whisk in the remaining ingredients. Spread this mixture evenly over the filling. 5. Place the pan in the air fryer basket and bake for 20 minutes, or until the topping is crispy and golden brown. Serve warm.

## Crumbly Coconut-Pecan Cookies

**Prep time: 10 minutes | Cook time: 25 minutes | Serves 10**

85 g coconut flour

85 g extra-fine almond flour

½ teaspoon baking powder

⅓ teaspoon baking soda

3 eggs plus an egg yolk, beaten

175 ml coconut oil, at room temperature

125 g unsalted pecan nuts, roughly chopped

150 g monk fruit, or equivalent sweetener

¼ teaspoon freshly grated nutmeg

⅓ teaspoon ground cloves

½ teaspoon pure vanilla extract

½ teaspoon pure coconut extract

⅛ teaspoon fine sea salt

1. Preheat the air fryer to 190°C. Line the air fryer basket with baking paper. 2. Mix the coconut flour, almond flour, baking powder, and baking soda in a large mixing bowl. 3. In another mixing bowl, stir together the eggs and coconut oil. Add the wet mixture to the dry mixture. 4. Mix in the remaining ingredients and stir until a soft dough forms. 5. Drop about 2 tablespoons of dough on the baking paper for each cookie and flatten each biscuit until it's 1 inch thick. 6. Bake for about 25 minutes until the cookies are golden and firm to the touch. Remove from the basket to a plate. Let the cookies cool to room temperature and serve.

## Pecan Clusters

**Prep time: 10 minutes | Cook time: 8 minutes | Serves 8**

85 g whole shelled pecans

1 tablespoon salted butter, melted

2 teaspoons powdered

sweetener

½ teaspoon ground cinnamon

½ cup low-carb chocolate chips

1. In a medium bowl, toss pecans with butter, then sprinkle with sweetener and cinnamon. 2. Place pecans into ungreased air fryer basket. Adjust the temperature to 180°C and air fry for 8 minutes, shaking the basket two times during cooking. They will feel soft initially but get crunchy as they cool. 3. Line a large baking sheet with baking paper. 4. Place chocolate in a medium microwave-safe bowl. Microwave on high, heating in 20-second increments and stirring until melted. Place 1 teaspoon chocolate in a rounded mound on ungreased baking paper -lined baking sheet, then press 1 pecan into top, repeating with remaining chocolate and pecans. 5. Place baking sheet into refrigerator to cool at least 30 minutes. Once cooled, store clusters in a large, sealed container in refrigerator up to 5 days.

## Rhubarb and Strawberry Crumble

**Prep time: 10 minutes | Cook time: 12 to 17 minutes | Serves 6**

250 g sliced fresh strawberries

95 g sliced rhubarb

40 g granulated sugar

30 g quick-cooking oatmeal

25 g whole-wheat pastry flour,

or All-purpose flour

40 g packed light brown sugar

½ teaspoon ground cinnamon

3 tablespoons unsalted butter, melted

1. Insert the crisper plate into the basket and the basket into the unit. Preheat the unit to 190°C. 2. In a 6-by-2-inch round metal baking pan, combine the strawberries, rhubarb, and granulated sugar. 3. In a medium bowl, stir together the oatmeal, flour, brown sugar, and cinnamon. Stir the melted butter into this mixture until crumbly. Sprinkle the crumble mixture over the fruit. 4. Once the unit is preheated, place the pan into the basket. 5.Bake for 12 minutes then check the crumble. If the fruit is bubbling and the topping is golden brown, it is done. If not, resume cooking. 6. When the cooking is complete, serve warm.

## Indian Toast and Milk

**Prep time: 10 minutes | Cook time: 20 minutes | Serves 4**

305 g sweetened, condensed milk

240 ml evaporated milk

240 ml single cream

1 teaspoon ground cardamom, plus additional for garnish

1 pinch saffron threads

4 slices white bread

2 to 3 tablespoons ghee or butter, softened

2 tablespoons crushed pistachios, for garnish (optional)

1. In a baking pan, combine the condensed milk, evaporated milk, half-and-half, cardamom, and saffron. Stir until well combined. 2. Place the pan in the air fryer basket. Set the air fryer to 180°C for 15 minutes, stirring halfway through the cooking time. Remove the sweetened milk from the air fryer and set aside. 3. Cut each slice of bread into two triangles. Brush each side with ghee. Place the bread in the air fryer basket. Keeping the air fryer on 180°C cook for 5 minutes or until golden brown and toasty. 4. Remove the bread from the air fryer. Arrange two triangles in each of four wide, shallow bowls. Pour the hot milk mixture on top of the bread and let soak for 30 minutes. 5. Garnish with pistachios if using, and sprinkle with additional cardamom.

# Butter Flax Cookies

**Prep time: 25 minutes | Cook time: 20 minutes |**
**Serves 4**

115 g almond meal

2 tablespoons flaxseed meal

30 g monk fruit, or equivalent sweetener

1 teaspoon baking powder

A pinch of grated nutmeg

A pinch of coarse salt

1 large egg, room temperature.

110 g unsalted butter, room temperature

1 teaspoon vanilla extract

1. Mix the almond meal, flaxseed meal, monk fruit, baking powder, grated nutmeg, and salt in a bowl. 2. In a separate bowl, whisk the egg, butter, and vanilla extract. 3. Stir the egg mixture into dry mixture; mix to combine well or until it forms a nice, soft dough. 4. Roll your dough out and cut out with a cookie cutter of your choice. Bake in the preheated air fryer at 180°C for 10 minutes. Decrease the temperature to 160°C and cook for 10 minutes longer. Bon appétit!

# Chocolate Soufflés

**Prep time: 5 minutes | Cook time: 14 minutes |**
**Serves 2**

Butter and sugar for greasing the ramekins

85 g semi-sweet chocolate, chopped

55 g unsalted butter

2 eggs, yolks and white separated

3 tablespoons granulated sugar

½ teaspoon pure vanilla extract

2 tablespoons All-purpose flour

Icing sugar, for dusting the finished soufflés

Heavy cream, for serving

1. Butter and sugar two 6-ounce (170 g) ramekins. (Butter the ramekins and then coat the butter with sugar by shaking it around in the ramekin and dumping out any excess.) 2. Melt the chocolate and butter together, either in the microwave or in a double boiler. In a separate bowl, beat the egg yolks vigorously. Add the sugar and the vanilla extract and beat well again. Drizzle in the chocolate and butter, mixing well. Stir in the flour, combining until there are no lumps. 3. Preheat the air fryer to 160°C. 4. In a separate bowl, whisk the egg whites to soft peak stage (the point at which the whites can almost stand up on the end of your whisk). Fold the whipped egg whites into the chocolate mixture gently and in stages. 5. Transfer the batter carefully to the buttered ramekins, leaving about ½-inch at the top. (You may have a little extra batter, depending on how airy the batter is, so you might be able to squeeze out a third soufflé

if you want to.) Place the ramekins into the air fryer basket and air fry for 14 minutes. The soufflés should have risen nicely and be brown on top. (Don't worry if the top gets a little dark, you'll be covering it with icing sugar in the next step.) 6. Dust with icing sugar and serve immediately with heavy cream to pour over the top at the table.

# Coconut-Custard Pie

**Prep time: 10 minutes | Cook time: 20 to 23 minutes |**
**| Serves 4**

240 ml milk

40 g granulated sugar, plus 2 tablespoons

30 g scone mix

1 teaspoon vanilla extract

2 eggs

2 tablespoons melted butter

Cooking spray

50 g shredded coconut

1. Place all ingredients except coconut in a medium bowl. 2. Using a hand mixer, beat on high speed for 3 minutes. 3. Let sit for 5 minutes. 4. Preheat the air fryer to 160°C. 5. Spray a baking pan with cooking spray and place pan in air fryer basket. 6. Pour filling into pan and sprinkle coconut over top. 7. Cook pie for 20 to 23 minutes or until center sets.

# White Chocolate Cookies

**Prep time: 5 minutes | Cook time: 11 minutes |**
**Serves 10**

225 g unsweetened white chocolate

2 eggs, well beaten

170 g butter, at room temperature

95 g almond flour

30 g coconut flour

150 g granulated sweetener

2 tablespoons coconut oil

⅓ teaspoon grated nutmeg

⅓ teaspoon ground allspice

⅓ teaspoon ground anise star

¼ teaspoon fine sea salt

1. Preheat the air fryer to 180°C. Line the air fryer basket with baking paper. 2. Combine all the ingredients in a mixing bowl and knead for about 3 to 4 minutes, or until a soft dough forms. Transfer to the refrigerator to chill for 20 minutes. 3. Make the cookies: Roll the dough into 1-inch balls and transfer to baking paper-lined basket, spacing 2 inches apart. Flatten each with the back of a spoon. 4. Bake for about 11 minutes until the cookies are golden and firm to the touch. 5. Transfer to a wire rack and let the cookies cool completely. Serve immediately.

## Pineapple Galette

**Prep time: 15 minutes | Cook time: 40 minutes |**
**Serves 2**

¼ medium-size pineapple,
peeled, cored, and cut crosswise
into ¼-inch-thick slices
2 tablespoons dark rum, or
apple juice
1 teaspoon vanilla extract
½ teaspoon kosher, or coarse
sea salt

Finely grated zest of ½ lime
1 store-bought sheet puff pastry,
cut into an 8-inch round
3 tablespoons granulated sugar
2 tablespoons unsalted butter,
cubed and chilled
Coconut ice cream, for serving

1. In a small bowl, combine the pineapple slices, rum, vanilla, salt, and lime zest and let stand for at least 10 minutes to allow the pineapple to soak in the rum. 2. Meanwhile, press the puff pastry round into the bottom and up the sides of a cake pan and use the tines of a fork to dock the bottom and sides. 3. Arrange the pineapple slices on the bottom of the pastry in a more or less single layer, then sprinkle with the sugar and dot with the butter. Drizzle with the leftover juices from the bowl. Place the pan in the air fryer and bake at 150°C until the pastry is puffed and golden brown and the pineapple is lightly caramelized on top, about 40 minutes. 4. Transfer the pan to a wire rack to cool for 15 minutes. Unmold the galette from the pan and serve warm with coconut ice cream.

## Lime Bars

**Prep time: 10 minutes | Cook time: 33 minutes |**
**Makes 12 bars**

140 g blanched finely ground
almond flour, divided
40 g powdered sweetener,
divided

4 tablespoons salted butter,
melted
120 ml fresh lime juice
2 large eggs, whisked

1. In a medium bowl, mix together 110 g flour, 25 g sweetener, and butter. Press mixture into bottom of an ungreased round nonstick cake pan. 2. Place pan into air fryer basket. Adjust the temperature to 150°C and bake for 13 minutes. Crust will be brown and set in the middle when done. 3. Allow to cool in pan 10 minutes. 4. In a medium bowl, combine remaining flour, remaining sweetener, lime juice, and eggs. Pour mixture over cooled crust and return to air fryer for 20 minutes. Top will be browned and firm when done. 5.

Let cool completely in pan, about 30 minutes, then chill covered in the refrigerator 1 hour. Serve chilled.

## Oatmeal Raisin Bars

**Prep time: 15 minutes | Cook time: 15 minutes |**
**Serves 8**

20 g All-purpose flour
¼ teaspoon kosher, or coarse
sea salt
¼ teaspoon baking powder
¼ teaspoon ground cinnamon
30 g light brown sugar, lightly
packed

40 g granulated sugar
120 ml canola, or rapeseed oil
1 large egg
1 teaspoon vanilla extract
110 g quick-cooking oats
60 g raisins

1. Preheat the air fryer to 180°C. 2. In a large bowl, combine the All-purpose flour, kosher salt, baking powder, ground cinnamon, light brown sugar, granulated sugar, canola oil, egg, vanilla extract, quick-cooking oats, and raisins. 3. Spray a baking pan with nonstick cooking spray, then pour the oat mixture into the pan and press down to evenly distribute. Place the pan in the air fryer and bake for 15 minutes or until golden brown. 4. Remove from the air fryer and allow to cool in the pan on a wire rack for 20 minutes before slicing and serving.

## Vanilla and Cardamon Walnuts Tart

**Prep time: 5 minutes | Cook time: 13 minutes |**
**Serves 6**

240 ml coconut milk
60 g walnuts, ground
30 g powdered sweetener
30 g almond flour
55 g butter, at room temperature

2 eggs
1 teaspoon vanilla essence
¼ teaspoon ground cardamom
¼ teaspoon ground cloves
Cooking spray

1. Preheat the air fryer to 180°C. Coat a baking pan with cooking spray. 2. Combine all the ingredients except the oil in a large bowl and stir until well blended. Spoon the batter mixture into the baking pan. 3. Bake in the preheated air fryer for approximately 13 minutes. Check the tart for doneness: If a toothpick inserted into the center of the tart comes out clean, it's done. 4. Remove from the air fryer and place on a wire rack to cool. Serve immediately.

Printed in Great Britain
by Amazon

42877471R00044